I0393619

Accounting and Auditing Policy Committee

Management's Discussion and Analysis Best Practices Report

May 2011

NOTE: This illustrative report was prepared by the AAPC MD&A "best practices" task group. This report is not intended to reflect authoritative views of the FASAB or its staff. Official positions of the FASAB are determined only after extensive due process and deliberations.

MD&A Best Practices

Introduction

Statement of Federal Financial Accounting Concepts (SFFAC) 3 and Statement of Federal Financial Accounting Standards (SFFAS) 15 provide guidance and requirements for management's discussion and analysis (MD&A) in federal agency financial reports. The standards call for management to present a frank and concise analysis of performance and financial results.

The MD&A should provide management's view of actual current performance and financial results as well as expectations about the future. It should be grounded in facts and provide meaningful explanatory data rather than be a series of vague and/or generally positive statements or vignettes about the entity's successes. The MD&A should present a balanced discussion of negative as well as positive results, and it should relate financial results, especially costs, to performance and both to strategic goals.

The MD&A should be a communication vehicle rather than a compliance exercise . It should be concise, meaningful, and readily understandable. In addition to explaining why financial results changed during the reporting period, MD&A should explain how performance did or did not achieve planned results. To the extent the results have been affected by any change in the underlying goals or performance measures, the nature and effects of such changes upon the outcomes should also be discussed.

However, current federal MD&A generally tend not to meet expectations established in SFFAC 3 and SFFAS 15. They typically do not effectively summarize and communicate entity performance and financial results. For example:

- There is often excessive narrative description, rather than concise information focused on the "vital few" matters envisioned by the standards. Program vignettes are often offered in place of concise analysis.
- Large numbers of performance measures are often included, rather than a limited number of key measures that clearly communicate how well the entity is achieving its goals and objectives. Numerous internal, operational measures are often presented whose relationship to the "vital few" entity goals is unclear, and which are not meaningful to external users unfamiliar with the intricacies of daily internal operations. Again, the goal should be to present a balanced discussion of performance.
- Discussion of the financial statements is often limited to noting changes in account balances during the reporting period, which are fairly obvious on the face of the financial statements, rather than explaining the reasons for the changes in balances and financial results. Also, significant variances from the budget are often not identified or explained.

In addition, charts, graphs, photographs and other pertinent graphics are often used and when effectively designed and presented, can significantly enhance the quality of the MD&A. However, in many instances their full potential is not realized due to shortcomings in their presentation such as use of (1) excessively small text fonts or photographs, (2) shading that obscures the text it is intended to highlight, and (3) overly ambitious charts and graphs that attempt to present too much information and thereby become very difficult to understand.

These issues have contributed to a perception that the MD&A in federal financial reports, as currently presented, is not as useful as was originally envisioned.

It should be noted that the federal government is not alone in questioning the decision-usefulness of financial reports. Much has been written about the need to improve the decision-usefulness of financial reports, especially regarding forward-looking information. There is a general call for concise reports with less reiteration of innocuous data and more discussion about the future.

Purpose of this Report

By providing available examples of "best practices" from current federal MD&A, this report is intended to help preparers of federal MD&A achieve the objectives of the standards and avoid some of the pitfalls that in the past have prevented these MD&A's from achieving their full potential as a vehicle to effectively communicate important information about the entity's mission, operations, goals, challenges, financial results, and future. This report provides examples of selected sections of certain federal fiscal year 2009 MD&As which the Accounting and Auditing Policy Committee (AAPC) believes effectively captured the letter and spirit of the key elements of the standards. They provide excellent examples.

Structure of this Report

This report is the product of a federal task group under the auspices of the AAPC.[1] The AAPC is a permanent committee established by the FASAB. The AAPC's mission is to assist the federal government in improving financial reporting by timely identifying, discussing, and recommending solutions to accounting issues within the framework of existing authoritative literature.

This report provides ideas for improving federal MD&A. The techniques and practices used to implement the current and past performance initiatives that are discussed in this document are not mandatory guidance. They should be viewed as useful examples of techniques for MD&A to better communicate essential information about the entity's operations.

[1] See Appendix 2 for a list of the task group members.

MD&A Best Practices

The report is organized by the four MD&A section indicated in SFFAS 15 as follows:

- **MISSION AND ORGANIZATIONAL STRUCTURE;**
- **PERFORMANCE GOALS, OBJECTIVES, AND RESULTS;**
- **ANALYSIS OF FINANCIAL STATEMENTS AND STEWARDSHIP INFORMATION SECTION;**
- **ANALYSIS OF SYSTEMS, CONTROLS AND LEGAL COMPLIANCE.**
- **FORWARD-LOOKING INFORMATION;**
- **HIGH RISK;**
- **IMPROPER PAYMENTS; and**
- **TREND DATA.**

The following table lists the federal agencies from whose MD&A sections examples of best practices were selected and provides Web links to their FY 2009 financial reports that includes their MD&A.

Table 1 – Agency Examples by MD&A Section

MD&A Section	Agency Example of Best Practice	AAPC Rpt. Page No.	Web Link to PAR or AFR containing the MD&A
Overview	Commerce	7	http://www.osec.doc.gov/bmi/budget/FY09PAR.html
	Defense	13	http://comptroller.defense.gov/afr/index.html
	VA	15	http://www4.va.gov/budget/report
Mission and Organization	Defense	21	http://comptroller.defense.gov/afr/index.html
	FTC	28	http://ftc.gov/opp/gpra/index.shtm
	NASA	33	http://www.nasa.gov/news/budget/index.html
	PTO	39	http://www.uspto.gov/about/stratplan/index.jsp
Performance goals, Objectives, And Results	Commerce	43	http://www.osec.doc.gov/bmi/budget/FY09PAR.html
	Defense	44	http://comptroller.defense.gov/afr/index.html
	EPA	52	http://www.epa.gov/ocfo/par/2009par/index.htm
	FAA	54	http://www.faa.gov/about/plans_reports
	GSA	57	http://www.gsa.gov/portal/category/26534
	Justice	57	http://www.justice.gov/ag/annualreports/pr2009/TableofContents.htm
	VA	59	http://www4.va.gov/budget/report
	FHFA	61	http://www.fhfa.gov/Default.aspx?Page=136
Analysis of Financial Statements and Stewardship	Energy	66	http://www.energy.gov/about/budget.htm
	GSA	69	http://www.gsa.gov/portal/category/26534
	FAA	69	http://www.faa.gov/about/plans_reports
	SBA	80	http://www.sba.gov/aboutsba/budgetsplans/SERV_ABTSBA_BUDGET_2009AFR.html
Analysis of Systems, Controls and Legal Compliance	GSA	83	http://www.gsa.gov/portal/category/26534
	PTO	85	http://www.uspto.gov/about/stratplan/index.jsp
	USDA	90	http://www.ocfo.usda.gov/usdarpt/usdarpt.htm
Forward-looking Information	FHFA	96	http://www.fhfa.gov/Default.aspx?Page=136
	USPS	98	http://www.usps.com/financials/ar/welcome.htm
	PTO	101	http://www.uspto.gov/about/stratplan/index.jsp
	VA	105	http://www4.va.gov/budget/report
High Risk	Energy	111	http://www.cfo.doe.gov/cf12/2009parAFR.pdf
Improper Payments	SSA	113	http://www.ssa.gov/finance/2009/Complete%20MD&A.pdf
Trend Data	Treasury	114	http://www.treasury.gov/about/organizational-structure/offices/Mgt/Documents/09AFR_Treasury_Tagged_07.pdf
Appendix 1		117	Current Federal MD&A Standards
Appendix 2		124	MD&A Task Group Members

DISCLAIMER

The examples of best practices included in this report have been reproduced verbatim from agency fiscal year 2009 Management Discussions and Analysis. The AAPC is not responsible for any factual, editorial, or other errors they may contain. They are intended to provide users with illustrative examples of the basic form and content of the various sections of the MD&A as they may appear when prepared as intended by the standards. The examples, in aggregate, are not intended to illustrate how to satisfy all MD&A requirements. That is, there may be some requirements for which the guide contains no examples.

This guide is intended to assist federal entities in reporting their MD&A information in federal agency reports in accordance with federal accounting standards. This guide supplements relevant federal accounting standards, but is not a substitute for and does not take precedence over the accounting standards issued by FASAB.

The federal agency MD&A examples in this guide illustrate how several federal entities report their MD&A sections. However, the examples are for illustrative purposes only. The examples are not all-encompassing and agencies may identify other more useful and relevant MD&A reporting practices. The examples also do not cover all MD&A requirements outlined in SFFAC 3 or SFFAS 15.

MD&A OVERVIEW

In addition to the MD&A sections explicitly mentioned in SFFAS 15, MD&A may include a brief overview or executive summary explaining the MD&A. An overview section gives the reader a useful summary of what is to come. Some agencies include an overview or executive summary in the "mission and organizational structure" section of the MD&A.

The following are examples of overview or executive summary "best practices".

Commerce Department

The following is from the Commerce Department's introductory material for FY 2009,[2]which precedes the MD&A, and provides an overview.

THE DEPARTMENT AT LARGE

HISTORY AND ENABLING LEGISLATION
The Department of Commerce was originally established by Congressional Act on February 14, 1903 as the Department of Commerce and Labor (32 Stat. 826; 5 U.S.C. 591) and was subsequently renamed the U.S. Department of Commerce by President William H. Taft on March 4, 1913 (15 U.S.C. Section 1512). The defined role of the new Department was "to foster, promote, and develop the foreign and domestic commerce, the mining, manufacturing, and fishery industries of the United States."

MISSION
The Department of Commerce creates the conditions for economic growth and opportunity by promoting innovation, entrepreneurship, competitiveness, and stewardship.

PROGRAM BUREAUS

- Economic Development Administration (EDA)
- Economic Statistics Administration (ESA)
  - Bureau of Economic Analysis (BEA)
  - Census Bureau
- International Trade Administration (ITA)
- Bureau of Industry and Security (BIS)
- Minority Business Development Agency (MBDA)
- U.S. Patent and Trademark Office (USPTO)
- National Institute of Standards and Technology
  - National Technical Information Service (NTIS)
- National Telecommunication and Information Administration (NTIA)
- National Oceanic and Atmospheric Administration (NOAA)

[2] For the referenced agency's financial report (and MD&A), see Table 1 above.

STRATEGIC GOALS
Goal 1: Maximize U.S. competitiveness and enable economic growth for American industries, workers, and consumers ***Goal 2***: Promote U.S. innovation and industrial competitiveness ***Goal 3***: Promote environmental stewardship ***Management Integration Goal***: Achieve organizational and management excellence

EMPLOYEES
As of September 30, 2009, the Department had approximately 54,400 employees. The size of the Department will fluctuate in the next three years depending on the needs of the Census Bureau, growing to more than 140,000 employees in FY 2010.

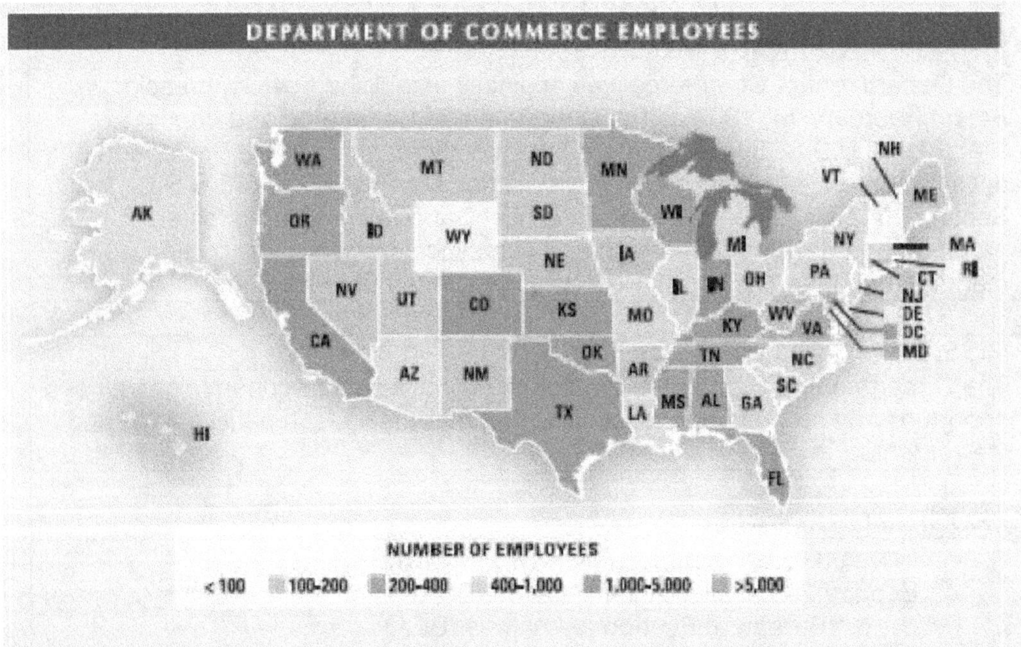

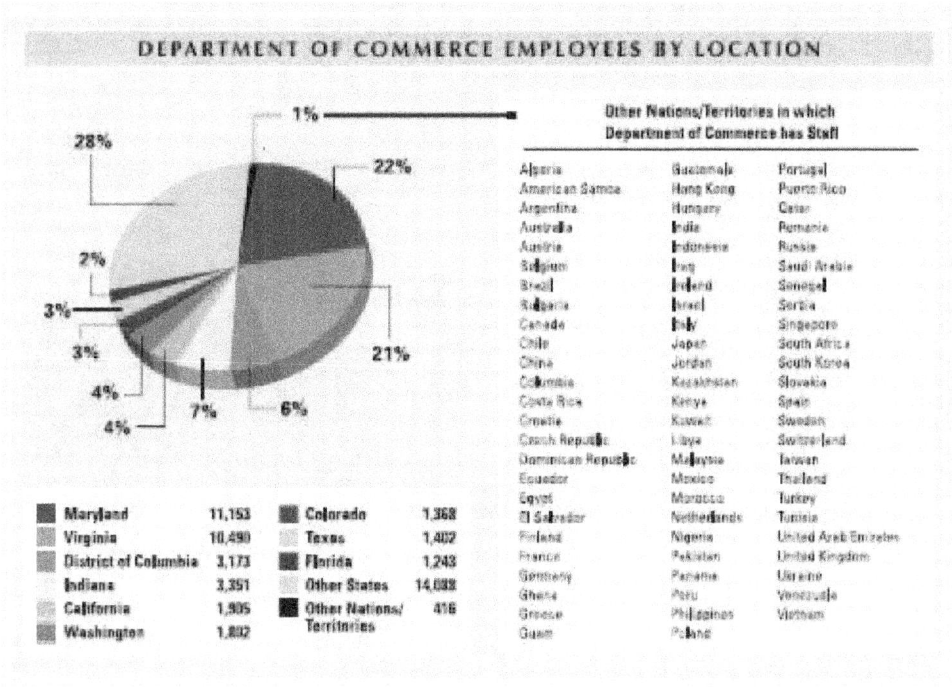

DEPARTMENT OF COMMERCE EMPLOYEES BY LOCATION
1%
28%
22%
2%
3%
3%
21%
4%
4%
7%
6%
Maryland 11,153
Virginia 10,490
District of Columbia 3,173
Indiana 3,351
California 1,905
Colorado 1,368
Florida 1,243
Other Nations/Territories 416
Other Nations/Territories in which Department of Commerce has Staff
Algeria
American Samoa
Argentina
Australia
Austria
Belgium
Brazil
Bulgaria
Canada
Chile
China
Columbia
Costa Rica
Croatia
Czech Republic
Dominican Republic
Ecuador
Egypt
El Salvador
Finland
France
Germany
Ghana
Greece
Guam
Guatemala
Hong Kong
Hungary
India
Indonesia
Iraq
Ireland
Israel
Italy
Japan
Jordan
Kazakhstan
Kenya
Kuwait
Libya
Malaysia
Mexico
Morocco
Netherlands
Nigeria
Pakistan
Panama
Peru
Philippines
Poland
Portugal
Puerto Rico
Qatar
Romania
Russia
Saudi Arabia
Senegal
Serbia
Singapore
South Africa
South Korea
Slovakia
Spain
Sweden
Switzerland
Taiwan
Thailand
Turkey
Tunisia
United Arab Emirates
United Kingdom
Ukraine
Venezuela
Vietnam

In the first several pages of the MD&A , the Commerce Department provides additional highlights as follows.

FY 2009 PERFORMANCE AND FINANCIAL HIGHLIGHTS

PERFORMANCE HIGHLIGHTS

In FY 2009, the Department met or exceeded 84 percent of its 123 performance targets. The Department has maintained a steady rate of performance from FY 2002 onward ranging from a low of 79 percent in FY 2003 to a high of 93 percent in FY 2007. Below are the funding amounts by strategic goal and financial highlights. Achieving results in each of the strategic goals furthers the Department's mission. This summary provides a snapshot of the targeted achievements. Discussions and highlights of successes are in the performance discussions of each performance goal.

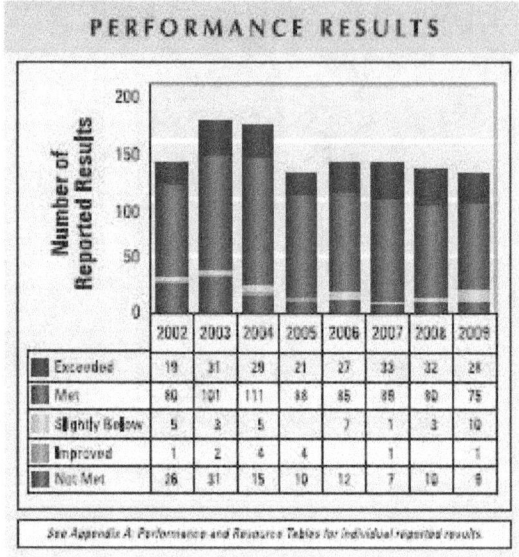

PERFORMANCE RESULTS

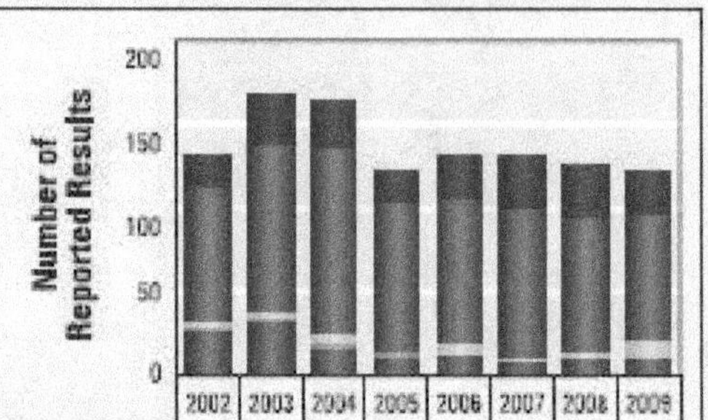

	2002	2003	2004	2005	2006	2007	2008	2009
Exceeded	19	31	29	21	27	33	32	28
Met	80	101	111	88	85	89	80	75
Slightly Below	5	3	5		7	1	3	10
Improved	1	2	4	4		1		1
Not Met	26	31	15	10	12	7	10	9

See Appendix A: Performance and Resource Tables for individual reported results.

(Dollars in Millions)[1]	Percentage Change	FY 2009	FY 2008
For the Years Ended September 30, 2009 and 2008			
Obligations by Strategic Goal:			
Strategic Goal 1: Maximize U.S. Competitiveness and Enable Economic Growth for American Industries, Workers, and Consumers[2]	+72.4%	$ 4,555.2	$ 2,642.4
Strategic Goal 2: Promote U.S. Innovation and Industrial Competitiveness	+3.8%	3,840.9	3,701.2
Strategic Goal 3: Promote Environmental Stewardship	+20.3%	5,094.1	4,234.4
Management Integration Goal: Achieve Organizational and Management Excellence	+17.1%	79.3	67.7
TOTAL OBLIGATIONS	+27.4%	$13,569.5	$10,645.7
Full Time Equivalents (FTEs) by Strategic Goal:			
Strategic Goal 1: Maximize U.S. competitiveness and enable economic growth for American industries, workers, and consumers[2]	+141.8%	29,266	12,103
Strategic Goal 2: Promote U.S. innovation and industrial competitiveness	+5.8%	12,798	12,096
Strategic Goal 3: Promote environmental stewardship	-4.8%	12,031	12,637
Management Integration Goal: Achieve Organizational and Management Excellence	+2.1%	297	291
TOTAL FTEs	+46.5%	54,392	37,127

Total Obligations

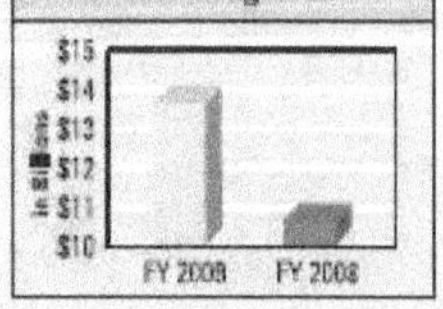

Total FTEs

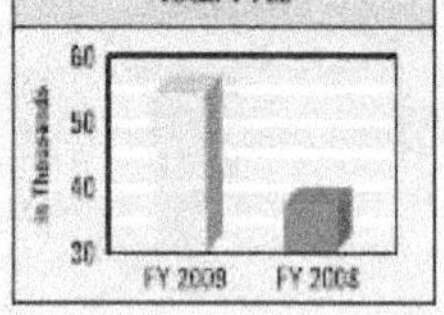

[1]Performance obligations may differ from obligations shown in financial reports because they do not include one-time funds for unexpected events (e.g., Hurricane Katrina) or reimbursable work that cannot be planned. In these cases, these obligations are not factored into bureau performance amounts.

[2]For Strategic Goal 1, the funding and FTE rose significantly in FY 2009 as a result of the Census Bureau's ramp up for the Decennial Census in 2010.

COMPOSITION OF THE DEPARTMENT'S FY 2009 ASSETS

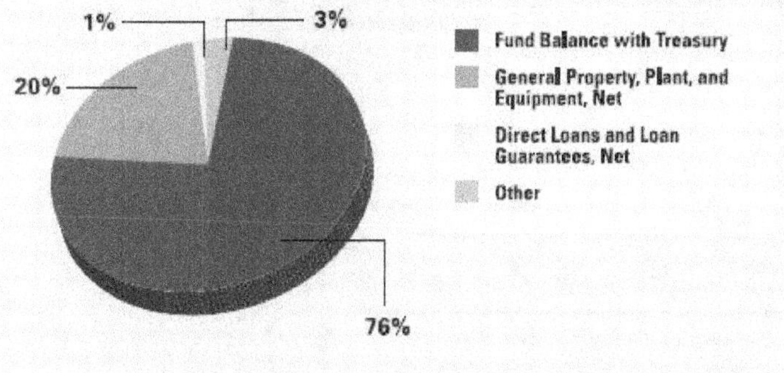

COMPOSITION OF THE DEPARTMENT'S FY 2009 LIABILITIES

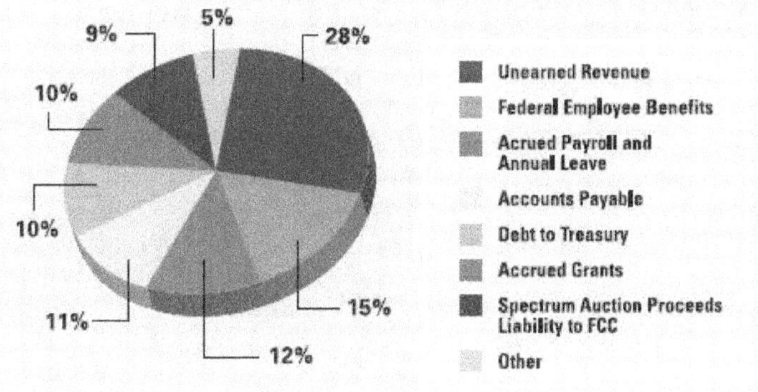

ASSETS

The Department had total assets of $34.0 billion as of September 30, 2009. This represents an increase of $240 million or 1 percent over total assets of $33.7 billion at September 30, 2008. Fund Balance with Treasury decreased $962 million or 4 percent, which primarily resulted from an increase in Advances and Prepayments of $583 million, and an increase in Construction-in-progress of $401 million, primarily related to satellites/weather systems personal property. General Property, Plant, and Equipment, Net increased $568 million or 9 percent, mainly due to the increase in Construction-in-progress. Other Assets increased $633 million, primarily due to a significant increase in Advances and Prepayments to other federal agencies for the National Telecommunications and Information Administration's (NTIA) Public Safety Interoperable Communications grant program and for work on the National Oceanic and Atmospheric Administration's (NOAA) Pacific Regional Center in Hawaii.

LIABILITIES

The Department had total liabilities of $4.6 billion as of September 30, 2009. This represents a decrease of $16.7 billion or 79 percent as compared to total liabilities of $21.5 billion at September 30, 2008. This decrease is mainly due to the large decrease of $16.9 billion in NTIA's Spectrum Auction Proceeds Liability to the Federal Communications Commission (FCC). This liability represents FCC auction proceeds for which licenses have not yet been granted by FCC. During FY 2009, the liability was primarily reduced by net auction proceeds for which licenses have been granted of $16.69 billion, and these net auction proceeds were recognized as a financing source on the FY 2009 Consolidated Statement of Changes in Net Position. Unearned Revenue decreased $107 million or 8 percent, mainly due to fewer patent filings and trademark applications received in FY 2009. Other Liabilities decreased $239 million or 50 percent, as a result of a large decrease of $141 million for accrued coupons for NTIA's Digital-to-Analog Converter Box Program, due to a significant decrease in the number of coupons issued during the third quarter of 2009 versus the third quarter of 2008.

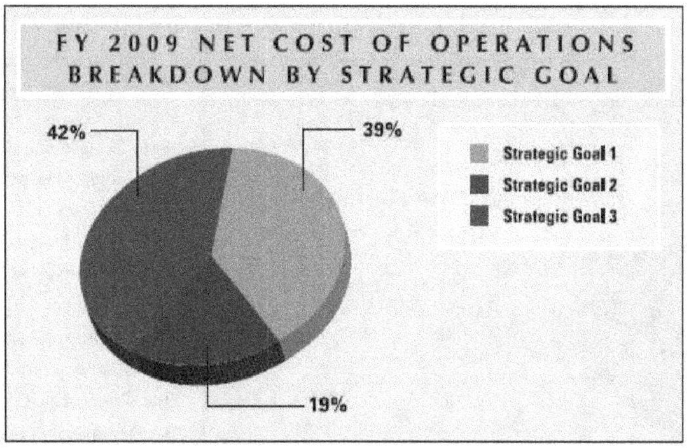

NET COST OF OPERATIONS

In FY 2009, Net Cost of Operations amounted to $9.8 billion, which consists of Gross Costs of $12.5 billion less Earned Revenue of $2.7 billion. Strategic Goal 1 includes Gross Costs of $4.1 billion related to maximizing U.S. competitiveness and enabling economic growth for American industries, workers, and consumers. Strategic Goal 2 includes Gross Costs of $4.0 billion related to promoting U.S. innovation and industrial competitiveness. Strategic Goal 3 includes Gross Costs of $4.4 billion related to promoting environmental stewardship. The Strategic Goal 1 increase in FY 2009 Net Cost of Operations over FY 2008 of $1.6 billion or 73 percent is primarily due to an increase in Gross Costs of $1.4 billion for Census Bureau's Decennial and Periodic Censuses major program. The Strategic Goal 2 increase in FY 2009 Net Cost of Operations over FY 2008 of $457 million or 32 percent is primarily due an increase in Gross Costs of $100 million for NTIA's Digital Television and Transition Public Safety Fund, which reflects increased costs primarily for the Digital-to-Analog Converter Box Program, and increased Gross Costs of $351 million provided by additional American Recovery and Reinvestment Act (ARRA) of 2009 funding for the Digital-to-Analog Converter Box Program.

Defense Department

In its FY 2009 MD&A, the Defense Department presents an effective summary of a complex organization as follows.

> **Fiscal Year 2009 Overview**
>
> The Defense Department is committed to executing our mission and responding to 21st Century national security requirements. In Fiscal Year (FY) 2009, the Department carried out its mission in many ways. We continued to engage in Operation Iraqi Freedom (OIF) military operations while executing a substantial portion of our responsible troop withdrawal from Iraq. In FY 2009, counter-Insurgency Operations (COIN) brigade combat teams (BCTs) in Iraq decreased from 14 to 12. Since the President announced the responsible withdrawal in May 2009, the Department saved $554 million in contractor costs, transferred 20,000 units of equipment to Afghanistan, and returned 10 percent of total OIF equipment to the U.S. The FY 2010 plans reflect the President's decision to decrease force levels to six Advisory and Assistance Brigades by August 31, 2010.
>
> While performing mission requirements in Iraq, we also increased our efforts in Operation Enduring Freedom (OEF) in Afghanistan. In FY 2009, we executed the President's decision to increase force levels from three to six BCTs with a Marine Expeditionary Brigade, a Stryker BCT, an Afghan Security Force training BCT, and additional supporting forces and capabilities. The additional 33,000 troops were critical in training Afghan Security Forces, bolstering International Security Assistance Force security in Regional Command East, retaking Helmand Province, and increasing security in Kandahar.
>
> While continuing to support OIF and OEF, the Department conducted numerous other military operations, including humanitarian efforts and relief operations throughout the world. For example, DoD provided disaster relief efforts in Taiwan, including supplies and airlift support, in response to the devastation caused by typhoon Marokot. In addition DoD provided humanitarian assistance, including building basic infrastructure, such as schools and roads, basic medical relief, and projects that enable host nations to prepare for disasters in as many as 80 countries.
>
> The Department depends on the Military Services to execute operations and in FY 2009 the Department took a number of steps to strengthen the Military Services. In FY 2009, the Army and Marine Corps successfully achieved their "grow the force" active military goals of 547,400 and 202,000 enlisted, respectively, more than two years ahead of schedule. The successful effort will allow the Army and Marine Corps to reduce the stress on their forces and will ultimately result in military members spending less time deployed. The Department also continued the growth of the special operations force level by over 5,000 military personnel. In addition to "growing the force," the Department created an additional regional command. The Africa Command (AFRICOM) was established on October 1, 2008, the first day of FY 2009. This command will greatly enhance the nation's focus on outreach and counterterrorism efforts in Africa.
>
> To carry out its key missions, the Department maintained focus and commitment to take care of its people: the all-volunteer military force, including the wounded Service members, military families, and civilians. Both military and civilian personnel received a 3.9 percent pay raise. The basic allowances for military housing and subsistence increased an average of 5.9 percent and 10.0 percent, respectively, to ensure that military families could cover increased costs. In recognition of the needs of our wounded warriors, the Department improved military health care facilities through funding initiatives such as warrior transition units. In addition, healthcare was provided for 9.3 million eligible beneficiaries in 59 inpatient medical facilities, more than 800

medical and dental clinics, as well as private sector care through the TRICARE program. To address the needs of military families, DoD invested in family support efforts such as childcare centers, schools, and youth programs.

The Department invested in new weapon system platforms and capabilities such as unmanned aerial vehicles, mine resistance ambush protected vehicles, and precision guided munitions to improve the nation's ability to combat unconventional threats. While investing in new weapon systems, the Department focused on aligning acquisitions to operational demands and requirements.

The Department implemented plans to improve acquisition effectiveness. We are committed to pursuing a number of acquisition excellence initiatives that address contracting and contract management issues, to include contracting in an expeditionary environment, addressing the Government Accountability Office's (GAO) high-risk area of interagency contracting, growing the contracting workforce, and increasing DoD organic acquisition management capability.

In addition to acquisition improvements, the Department continues to make improvements in financial management and audit readiness. The DoD established plans to improve business practices and internal controls to enhance visibility and accountability of its resources. The Department strengthened the business environment within the operational theater to increase effectiveness in terms of responsive mission support and better control over resources. To accomplish this, the Department formed a cross-functional team of senior leaders to ensure that the people, processes, and systems were in place at appropriate levels to provide management visibility and assurance over controls. The underlying goal is to provide support for improved mission effectiveness, enhanced personnel safety/security, reduced likelihood of loss of funds or erroneous payments, less rework, and better cost visibility and control. By applying lessons learned from prior theater experience, the Department hopes to develop an enhanced capability for future contingencies and theater operations.

In FY 2009, the Department established plans for continued management reform organized around high-priority performance goals. These plans will:

- Increase energy efficiencies
- Reform the personnel security clearance process
- Execute Virtual Lifetime Electronic Record (VLER) milestones
- Streamline the hiring process
- Spend American Recovery and Reinvestment Act (ARRA) funds quickly and effectively
- Provide effective business operations and ensure logistics support to Overseas Contingency Operations (OCO)
- Increase the audit readiness of individual DoD components
- Reform the DoD acquisition process
- Enhance the security cooperation workforce

In summary, during FY 2009, the Secretary emphasized the strategic priorities of taking care of our people; reshaping and modernizing the force; reforming how the Department buys equipment and services; and supporting the troops in the field.

Veterans Affairs

Some MD&A presentations provide a Web-based Performance and Accountability Report (PAR) with hyperlinks to MD&A sections (and other sections of its PAR). Several agencies provide similar Web pages, which are very helpful. See Table 1 above for the Web addresses. The Department of Veteran's Affairs (VA)'s PAR and MD&A is an outstanding example of this approach.

Regarding the overview section, the VA begins its MD&A with a "performance scorecard", which is followed in due course by a concise "performance overview" as follows.

Performance Scorecard

Color coding for FY 2009 Results: Target Achieved; Target Missed – Small Extent; Target Missed – Great Extent

Strategic Goals	Key Performance Measures (page references)	FY 2008 Recap Targets	FY 2008 Recap Results	FY 2009 Recap Targets	FY 2009 Recap Results	Target Achieved? Yes	Target Achieved? No	Improved From FY 2008? Yes/No/Same	Measure Type
Strategic Goal #1 Restoration and Improved Quality of Life for Disabled Veterans	National accuracy rate for compensation rating claims (pp. II-12 & 134)	90%	86%	90%	83%*		No	No	Output
	Compensation & Pension rating-related actions — average days to complete (pp. II-10 & 134) (Also supports SG #3)	169	179	168	161	Yes		Yes	Output
	Rating-related compensation actions - average days pending (pp. II-11 & 134)	120	121	116	117		No	Yes	Output
	Rehabilitation Rate (General) (pp. II-17 & 134)	75%	76%	76%	74%		No	No	Outcome
	Average days to complete Dependency and Indemnity Compensation actions (pp. II-21 & 134)	118	121	115	109	Yes		Yes	Output
Strategic Goal #2 Smooth Transition to Civilian Life	Average days to complete education claims								
	Original claims (pp. II-30 & 134)	24	19	24	26		No	No	Output
	Supplemental claims (pp. II-31 & 134)	11	9	10	13		No	No	Output
Strategic Goal #3 Honoring, Serving, and Memorializing Veterans	Percent of patients rating VA health care service as very good or excellent: - Inpatient (pp. II-43 & 136)	79%	79%	Baseline	62%*				Outcome
	- Outpatient (pp. II-44 & 136)	79%	78%	Baseline	56%*				Outcome
	Percent of primary care appointments completed within 30 days of the desired date (pp. II-39 & 136)	97%	99%	97%	99%*	Yes		Same	Output
	Percent of specialty care appointments completed within 30 days of the desired date (pp. II-40 & 136)	95%	98%	95%	98%*	Yes		Same	Output
	Percent of new patient appointments completed within 30 days of the create date (pp. II-41 & 136)	Baseline	89%	92%	90%*		No	Yes	Output
	Percent of unique patients waiting more than 30 days beyond the desired appointment date (pp. II-42 & 136)	Baseline	8%	6%	8%*		No	Same	Output

Performance Scorecard

Color coding for FY 2009 Results: Target Achieved; Target Missed – Small Extent; Target Missed – Great Extent

Strategic Goals	Key Performance Measures (page references)	FY 2008 Recap Targets	FY 2008 Recap Results	FY 2009 Recap Targets	FY 2009 Recap Results	Target Achieved? Yes	Target Achieved? No	Improved From FY 2008? Yes/No/Same	Measure Type
Strategic Goal #3 (continued) – Honoring, Serving, and Memorializing Veterans	Clinical Practice Guidelines Index III (pp. II-37 & 136)	85%	84%	86%	86%*	Yes		Yes	Outcome
	Prevention Index IV (pp. II-38 & 138)	88%	88%	89%	89%*	Yes		Yes	Outcome
	Non-institutional, long-term care average daily census (pp. II-45 & 138)	N/Av	54,053	72,352	71,944*		No	Yes	Output
	Pension maintenance claims — average days to complete (pp. II-50 & 138)	84	119	85	101		No	Yes	Output
	National accuracy rate for pension maintenance claims (pp. II-51 & 138)	92%	93%	94%	94%*	Yes		Yes	Output
	Average number of days to process Traumatic Injury Protection Insurance disbursements (pp. II-55 & 138)	5.0	2.5	5.0	2.9	Yes		No	Output
	Percent of Veterans served by a burial option within a reasonable distance (75 miles) of their residence (pp. II-60 & 140)	83.7%	84.2%	86.9%	87.4%	Yes		Yes	Outcome
	Percent of respondents who rate the quality of service provided by the national cemeteries as excellent (pp. II-61 & 140)	97%	94%	98%	95%		No	Yes	Outcome
	Percent of graves in national cemeteries marked within 60 days of interment (pp. II-66 & 140)	95%	93%	95%	95%	Yes		Yes	Output
	Percent of applications for headstones and markers that are processed within 20 days for the graves of Veterans who are not buried in national cemeteries (pp. II-67 & 140)	75%	95%	90%	93%	Yes		No	Output
	Default Resolution Rate (pp. II-72 & 140)	N/Av	N/Av	56.5%	66.4%	Yes		N/A	Outcome
Strategic Goal #4 – Contributing to the Nation's Well-Being	Progress towards development of one new treatment for post-traumatic stress disorder (3 milestones over 3 years) (pp. II-80 & 140)	80%	80%	87%	80%*		No	Same	Outcome
	Percent of respondents who rate national cemetery appearance as excellent (pp. II-90 & 142)	99%	98%	99%	98%		No	Same	Outcome

How We Measure Performance

VA employs a **five-tiered performance management framework** to measure performance.

Term	*Definition*
Strategic Goals	The Department's long-term outcomes as detailed in its Strategic Plan and articulated through four strategic goals and one enabling goal.
Strategic Objectives	Broad operational focus areas designed to achieve strategic goals. The Department has 21 strategic objectives.
Performance Measures	Specific measurable indicators used to measure progress towards achievement of strategic objectives. The Department uses different types of measures (i.e., outcome, output, and efficiency) to evaluate its performance and progress.
Performance Targets	Associated with specific performance measures, these are quantifiable expressions of desired performance/success levels to be achieved during a given fiscal year.
Strategic Targets	Also associated with specific performance measures, these are quantifiable expressions of optimum success levels to be achieved; they are "*stretch goals*" that VA strives for in the long-term.

VA's 21 strategic objectives are supported by 104 performance measures, 26 of which were identified by VA's senior leadership as **mission critical**. The Department's performance measures are a mix of program outcomes that measure the impact that VA programs have on the lives of Veterans and their families, program outputs that measure activities undertaken to manage and administer these programs, and program efficiency that measures the cost of delivering an output or desired outcome.

Key Features of the FY 2009 Report

VA's PAR includes several features designed to give our stakeholders more complete information on VA's performance and activities.

Key Feature	*Benefit to VA's Stakeholders*
Cost Per Measure Data	The Department is furthering its integration of performance and budget information. As part of this effort, this year's PAR includes information on the cost of achieving performance targets for *nine* measures. We provide this in addition to cost estimates provided by strategic goal and objective, respectively.
Major Management Challenges	This year's report improves how major management challenges are presented. VA's response to each challenge is presented in an easy-to-read tabular format providing an estimated resolution date, a responsible official, a summary of actions taken, milestones planned for FY 2010, and anticipated impacts of actions planned. In addition, the presentation now divides the response into three categories: People, Process, and Policy. Together these elements provide a comprehensive analysis of the challenges facing the Department and what VA is doing to address them.
Web Links	This year's PAR lists more VA Web links compared to last year's PAR.
Data Quality Information	This year's report contains more robust and detailed information on how VA verifies the quality of its performance results data. The report's Key Measures Data Table and the Assessment of Data Quality sections have been restructured to provide more comprehensive data quality information.
Dashboard Style Tables	Selected tables now include more dashboard-like features that convey performance results using easy-to-read tables and "traffic light" color coding to help the reader more quickly and clearly assess VA performance results.
VA Snapshots	Snapshots are short vignettes that give the reader an easy way to understand VA through human interest stories.
Strategic Objective Measures Recap	Our strategic objective chapters in Part II now include a recap of all measures and associated results for a given objective including a statistical recap.

2009 Performance -- *A Department-Level Summary*

Key Measures -- *Continuity and Type*: Key measures are those that measure mission-critical activities. As of FY 2009, 25 of VA's 26 key measures have been in place for at least 5 years. This provides the Department's leadership with the ability to track significant performance trends over time and to make strategic adjustments when necessary.

Performance Results: *Key vs. All Measures:* The chart below shows how well VA performed in meeting its performance targets. As shown, VA achieved the target for 50 percent of its key measures and 64 percent of all measures. In addition, for key measures, 21 percent of the targets were not achieved, but performance improved from 2008. Further details on performance by goal and objective are provided on the following pages.

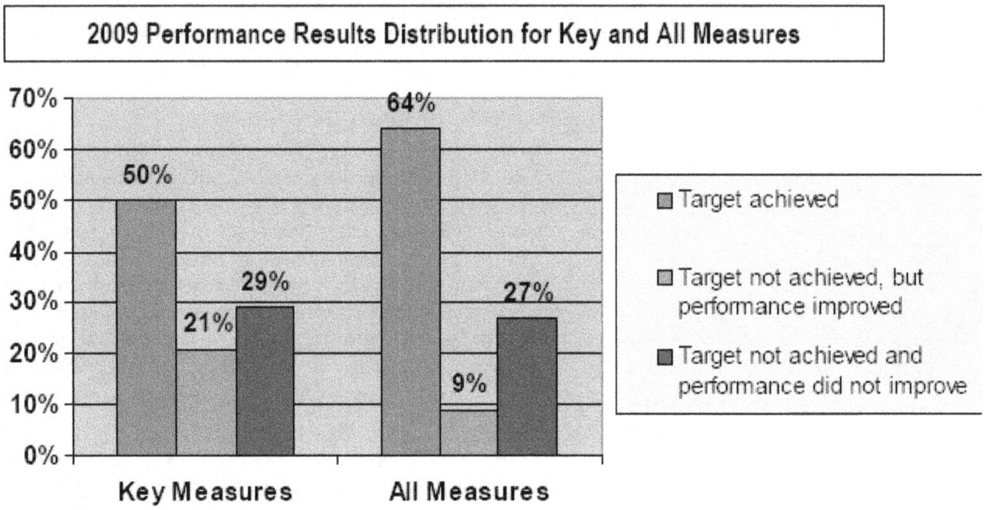

Performance Trends: *All Measures:* The chart below shows how well VA performed in meeting its performance targets for all of its measures since 2004. Trend analysis should be considered in light of yearly changes to performance targets and, to a lesser extent, changes to the numbers and types of measures.

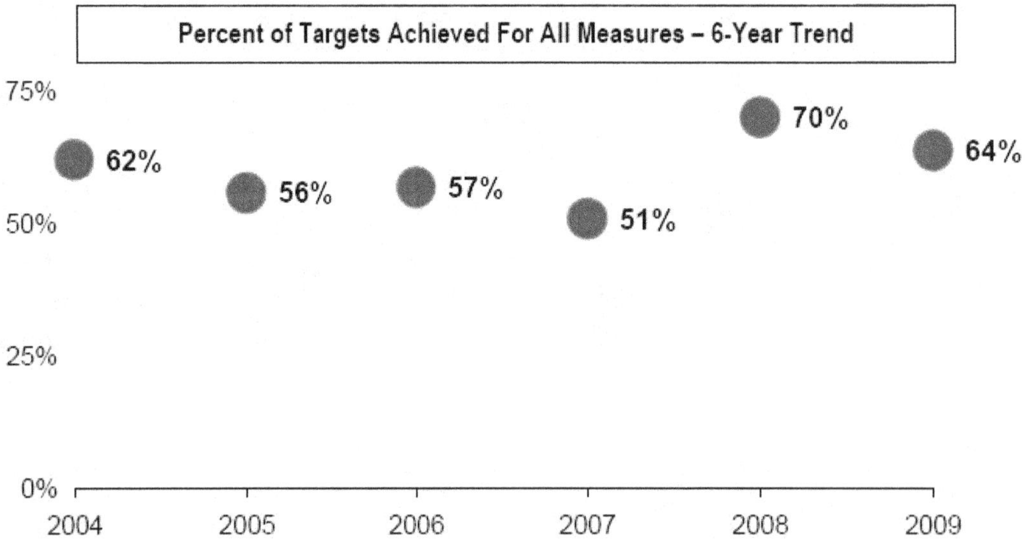

MISSION AND ORGANIZATIONAL STRUCTURE

Regarding the four MD&A sections listed in SFFAS 15, the ***mission and organizational structure*** section should be concise and easily understood. Well-designed graphics help a great deal. Best practices for the mission and organizational structure follow, starting with the Defense Department.

Defense Department

The Defense Department's MD&A concise and easily understood description of a complex organization is shown on the following pages.

Organization

The Department must be effectively structured to make best use of its resources. Since the creation of the Continental Army in 1775, the U.S. military has evolved to become a global presence. The DoD was created by the National Security Act of 1947 by combining the Department of War and the Department of the Navy and was called the National Military Establishment; it became the DoD when the act was amended in 1949. Under the act, the Secretary of Defense, who is appointed by the President with the consent of the Senate, supervises the entire military. Under the Secretary of Defense is the Joint Chiefs of Staff. The Joint Chiefs consist of a chairperson, who holds the grade of General or Admiral, the heads of the three main Military Departments, and the Commandant of the Marine Corps. The Secretary of the Army, the Secretary of the Navy, and the Secretary of the Air Force were subordinated to give the Secretary of Defense full Cabinet authority over the Department.

The DoD embraces the core values of all successful organizations: leadership, professionalism, and technical knowledge. Its employees are dedicated to duty, integrity, ethics, honor, courage, and loyalty. Figure 1-3 shows how the Department is structured.

The Secretary and the Office of the Secretary

The Secretary of Defense and the Office of the Secretary of Defense are responsible for the formulation and oversight of America's defense strategy and policy. The Office of the Secretary of Defense supports the Secretary in policy development, planning, resource management, and fiscal and program evaluation.

Figure 1-3

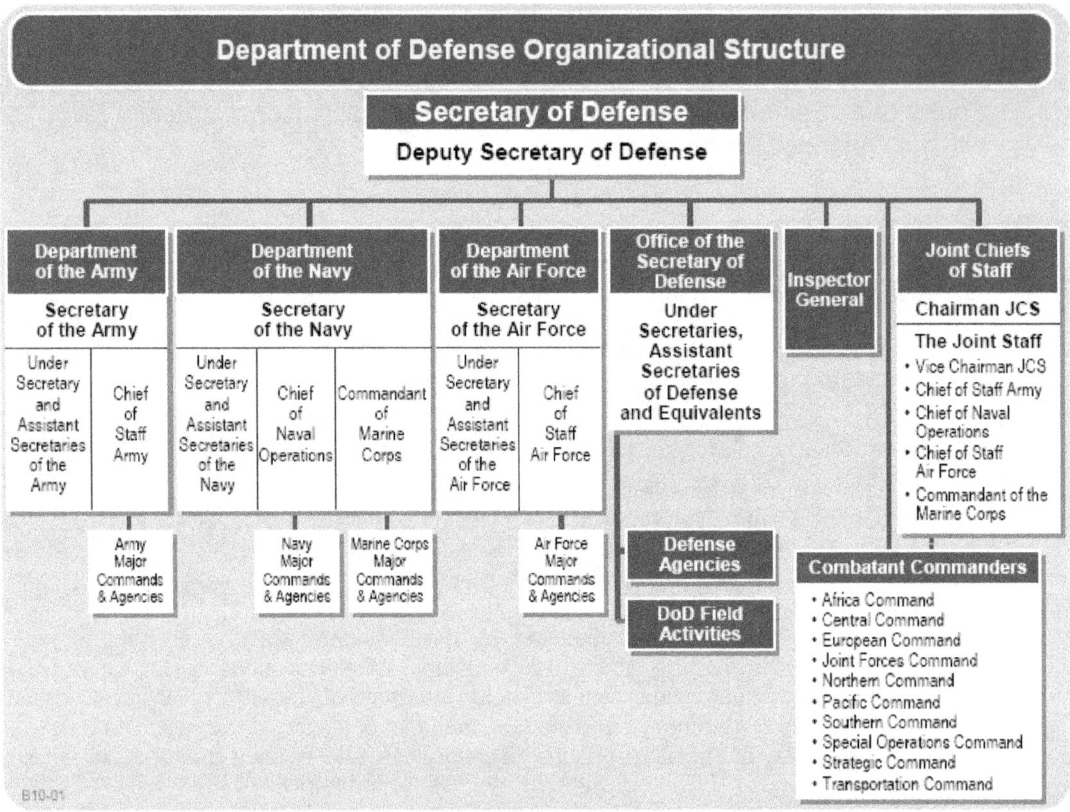
Department of Defense Organizational Structure
Secretary of Defense
Deputy Secretary of Defense
Department of the Army
Secretary of the Army
Under Secretary and Assistant Secretaries of the Army
Chief of Staff Army
Army Major Commands & Agencies
Department of the Navy
Secretary of the Navy
Under Secretary and Assistant Secretaries of the Navy
Chief of Naval Operations
Commandant of Marine Corps
Navy Major Commands & Agencies
Marine Corps Major Commands & Agencies
Department of the Air Force
Secretary of the Air Force
Under Secretary and Assistant Secretaries of the Air Force
Chief of Staff Air Force
Air Force Major Commands & Agencies
Office of the Secretary of Defense
Under Secretaries, Assistant Secretaries of Defense and Equivalents
Defense Agencies
DoD Field Activities
Inspector General
Joint Chiefs of Staff
Chairman JCS
The Joint Staff
• Vice Chairman JCS
• Chief of Staff Army
• Chief of Naval Operations
• Chief of Staff Air Force
• Commandant of the Marine Corps
Combatant Commanders
• Africa Command
• Central Command
• European Command
• Joint Forces Command
• Northern Command
• Pacific Command
• Southern Command
• Special Operations Command
• Strategic Command
• Transportation Command

Military Departments

The Military Departments consist of the Army, the Navy (of which the Marine Corps is a component), and the Air Force. In wartime, the U.S. Coast Guard becomes a special component of the Navy; otherwise, it is a maritime service within the Department of Homeland Security. The Military Departments organize, train, and equip America's military forces. When the President and Secretary of Defense determine that military action is required, these trained and ready forces are assigned to a Combatant Command responsible for conducting the military operations.

The Military Departments include Active Duty, Reserve, and National Guard forces. Active Duty forces are full-time Military Service Members. The Reserves, when directed by Congress or Presidential declaration, support the active forces. They are an extension of the Active Duty personnel and perform similarly when called into service. The Reserves may also be called upon to conduct counterdrug operations, provide disaster aid, and perform other peacekeeping missions. The National Guard has a unique dual mission, with both Federal and State responsibilities. In peacetime, the Governor of each respective State or territory commands the Guard. The Governor can call the Guard into action during local or Statewide emergencies, such as storms, wild fires, or civil disturbances. When ordered to active duty for mobilization or called into Federal Service for emergencies, units of the Guard are under the control of the appropriate DoD Military Department. The Guard and Reserve are recognized as indispensable and integral parts of our Nation's defense from the earliest days of a conflict.

- **Department of the Army.** The mission of the Department of the Army is to provide organized, trained, and equipped ground and combat support forces to the Combatant Commanders in support of National Security and Defense Strategies. The Army is committed to remaining the world's preeminent land power – relevant and ready at all times to serve the nation and support our allies.
- **Department of the Navy.** The mission of the Department of the Navy is to organize, train, and equip combat-ready Navy and Marine Corps forces capable of winning wars, deterring aggression and maintaining freedom of the seas.
- **Department of the Air Force.** The mission of the United States Air Force is to organize, train, and equip forces to fly, fight, and win in air, space, and cyberspace. The Air Force also strives to preserve the peace and security of the U.S. by providing the Combatant Commanders air-combat, air-service, aerospace, missile, and airlift forces.
- **Defense Agencies and Defense Field Activities.** Defense Agencies and DoD Field Activities provide support services commonly used throughout the Department. For example, the Defense Finance and Accounting Service (DFAS) provides accounting and payroll services, and contractor and vendor payments. Another example is the Defense Logistics Agency (DLA), which provides logistics support and supplies to all DoD activities.

Combatant Commands

The Secretary of Defense exercises his authority over how the military is trained and equipped through the Service secretaries; however, the Secretary of Defense uses a totally different method to exercise his authority to deploy troops and exercise military power. This latter authority is directed, with the advice of the Chairman of the Joint Chiefs of Staff, to the ten Combatant Commands who are responsible for conducting DoD missions around the world (Figure 1-4).

The combatant commanders are the direct link from the military forces to the President and the Secretary of Defense.

Six commanders have specific mission objectives for geographical areas of responsibility as depicted in Figure 1-5.

- **U.S. Northern Command (USNORTHCOM)** is responsible for North America.
- **U.S. Pacific Command (USPACOM)** is responsible for Northeast Asia, South Asia, and Southeast Asia, as well as Oceania.
- **U.S. European Command (USEUCOM)** is responsible for activities in Europe, Greenland, and Russia.
- **U.S. Southern Command (USSOUTHCOM)** is responsible for Central and South America, and the Caribbean.
- **U.S. Africa Command (USAFRICOM)** is responsible for all of Africa, with the exception of Egypt.
- **U.S. Central Command (USCENTCOM)** is responsible for the Middle East, several of the former Soviet republics, and Egypt. This Command is bears primary responsibility for Operation Enduring Freedom in Afghanistan and Operation Iraqi Freedom.

Figure 1-4

Figure 1-5

Four commanders have worldwide mission responsibilities, each focused on a particular function:

- **U.S. Strategic Command (USSTRATCOM)** is responsible for providing global deterrence capabilities and synchronizing DoD efforts to combat weapons of mass destruction worldwide.
- **U.S. Special Operations Command (USSOCOM)** is responsible for providing fully capable Special Operations Forces to defend the U.S. and its interests and synchronize planning of global operations against terrorist networks.
- **U.S. Transportation Command (USTRANSCOM)** is responsible for moving military equipment, supplies, and personnel around the world in support of operations.
- **U.S. Joint Forces Command (USJFCOM)** is responsible for developing future concepts for joint warfighting.

Federal Trade Commission

The Federal Trade Commission's mission and organizational structure section is concise and easily grasped as follows.

Mission and Organization

The work of the Federal Trade Commission (FTC) is critical to protecting and strengthening free and open markets and promoting informed consumer choice, both in the United States and around the world. The FTC performs its mission through the use of a variety of tools, including law enforcement, rulemaking, research, studies on marketplace trends and legal developments, and consumer and business education.

FTC's Vision

A U.S. economy characterized by vigorous competition among producers and consumer access to accurate information, yielding high-quality products at low prices and encouraging efficiency, innovation, and consumer choice.

FTC's Mission

To prevent business practices that are anticompetitive or deceptive or unfair to consumers; to enhance informed consumer choice and public understanding of the competitive process; and to accomplish these missions without unduly burdening legitimate business activity.

The FTC: Our Purpose and History

Consumers and businesses are likely to be more familiar with the work of the FTC than they think. In the consumer protection area, the care labels in clothes, product warranties, or stickers showing the energy costs of home appliances illustrate information that is required by the FTC. Likewise, businesses must be familiar with the laws requiring truthful advertising and protecting consumers' personally identifiable information and sensitive health information. These laws are administered by the FTC.

Each year, more people around the globe have come to understand that the competition among independent businesses is good for consumers, the businesses themselves, and the economy. Competitive markets yield lower prices and better quality goods and services, and a vigorous marketplace provides the incentive and opportunity for the development of new ideas and innovative products and services. Many of the laws governing competition also are administered by the FTC.

The FTC has a long tradition of maintaining a competitive marketplace for both consumers and businesses. When the FTC was created in 1914, its purpose was to prevent unfair methods of competition in commerce as part of the battle to "bust the trusts." Over the years, the Congress passed additional laws giving the agency greater authority over anticompetitive practices. In 1938, the Congress passed a broad prohibition against "unfair and deceptive acts or practices." Since then, the FTC also has been directed to administer a wide variety of other consumer protection laws and regulations, including the Telemarketing Sales Rule, the Identity Theft Act, and the Equal Credit Opportunity Act.

FTC History and Laws

The FTC had its genesis in the Supreme Court's 1911 decision in the Standard Oil case (Standard Oil Co. v. U.S., 221 U.S. 1 (1911)). In the aftermath of that decision, Congress determined to create an administrative agency that would be directed to prevent "unfair methods of competition;" to give definition to that general prohibition; and to use a number of quasi-judicial powers to enforce that prohibition. The FTC Act was later amended to prohibit unfair or deceptive acts or practices. Since its creation in 1914, Congress has substantially increased the FTC's enforcement responsibilities with respect to both of its goals, protecting consumers and maintaining competition. The FTC currently has enforcement and administrative responsibilities under 46 laws. For a description and further information on each law see http://www.ftc.gov/ogc/stats.shtm.

FISCAL YEAR
2009

Our Organization

The FTC is an independent agency that reports to the Congress on its actions. These actions include pursuing vigorous and effective law enforcement; advancing consumers' interests by sharing its expertise with federal and state legislatures and U.S. and international government agencies; developing policy and research tools through hearings, workshops, and conferences; and creating practical and plain-language educational programs for consumers and businesses in a global marketplace with constantly changing technologies.

The FTC is headed by a Commission composed of five commissioners, nominated by the President and confirmed by the Senate, each serving a seven-year term. The President chooses one commissioner to act as Chairman. No more than three commissioners can be from the same political party. Jon Leibowitz was designated to serve as Chairman of the FTC on March 2, 2009, by President Barack H. Obama. Leibowitz was previously sworn in as a Commissioner on September 3, 2004, following his nomination by the President and confirmation by the U.S. Senate. At the end of the fiscal year, the commissioners were Pamela Jones Harbour, William E. Kovacic, and J. Thomas Rosch. The fifth commissioner position was vacant.

The FTC's mission is carried out by three bureaus: the Bureau of Consumer Protection, the Bureau of Competition, and the Bureau of Economics. Work is aided by offices, including the Office of General Counsel, the Office of Inspector General, the Office of International Affairs, the Office of the Executive Director, and seven regions.

Federal Trade Commission Organization Chart

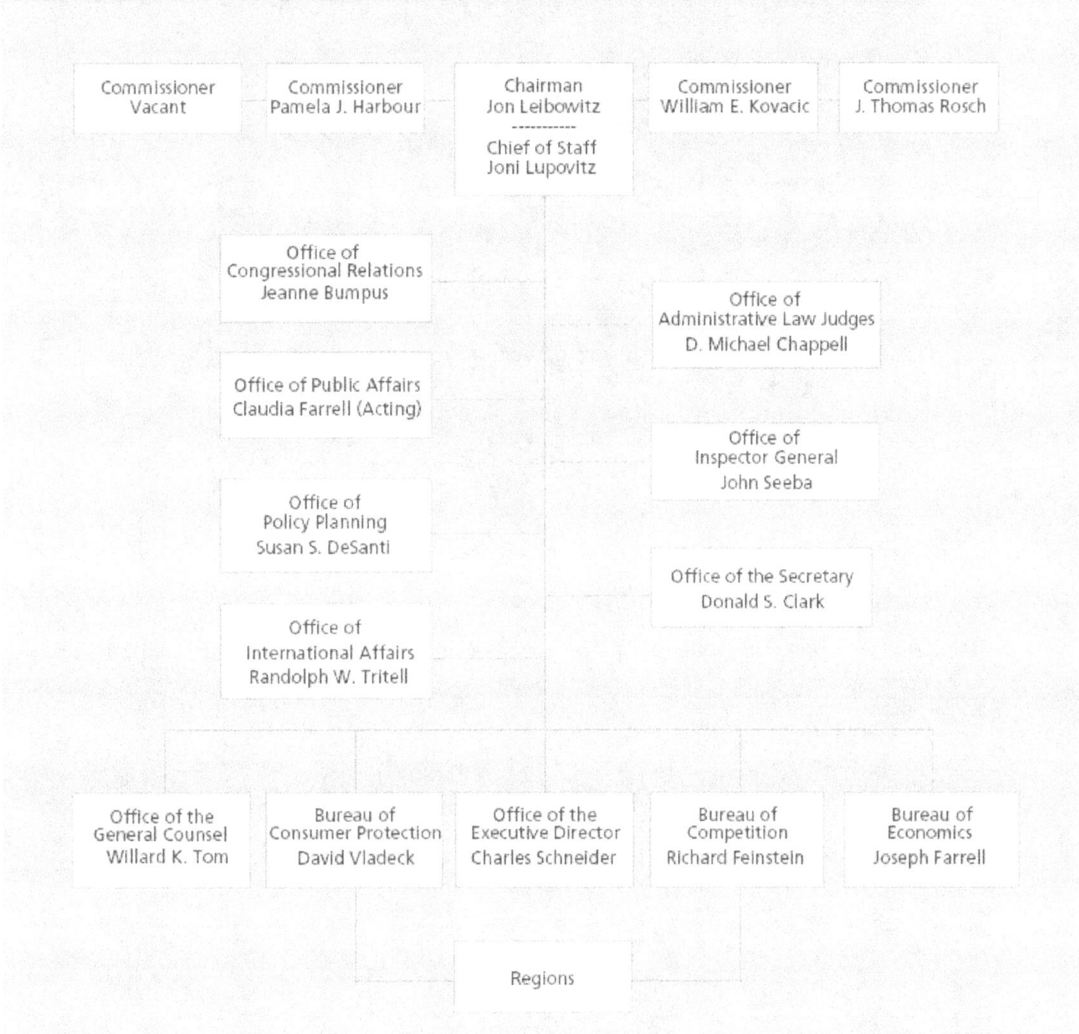
Commissioner
Vacant
Commissioner
Pamela J. Harbour
Chairman
Jon Leibowitz
Chief of Staff
Joni Lupovitz
Commissioner
William E. Kovacic
Commissioner
J. Thomas Rosch
Office of
Congressional Relations
Jeanne Bumpus
Office of
Administrative Law Judges
D. Michael Chappell
Office of Public Affairs
Claudia Farrell (Acting)
Office of
Inspector General
John Seeba
Office of
Policy Planning
Susan S. DeSanti
Office of the Secretary
Donald S. Clark
Office of
International Affairs
Randolph W. Tritell
Office of the
General Counsel
Willard K. Tom
Bureau of
Consumer Protection
David Vladeck
Office of the
Executive Director
Charles Schneider
Bureau of
Competition
Richard Feinstein
Bureau of
Economics
Joseph Farrell
Regions

The agency is headquartered in Washington, DC, and operates with seven regions across the United States. The graphic below illustrates the locations of the FTC regions.

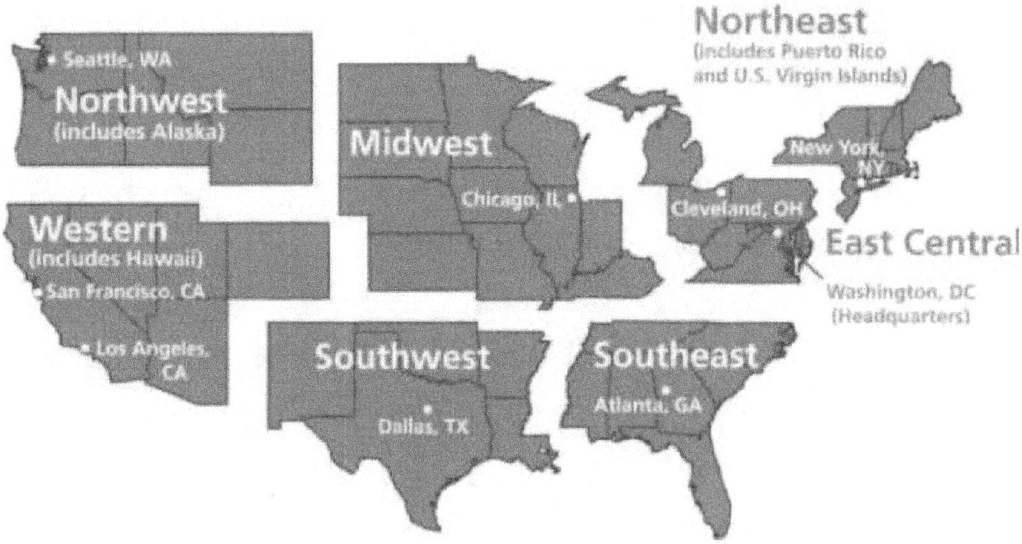

Our People

The FTC's workforce is its greatest asset. The agency's workforce consists of over 1,100 civil service employees dedicated to addressing the major concerns of American consumers. The graph below shows workforce composition by category.

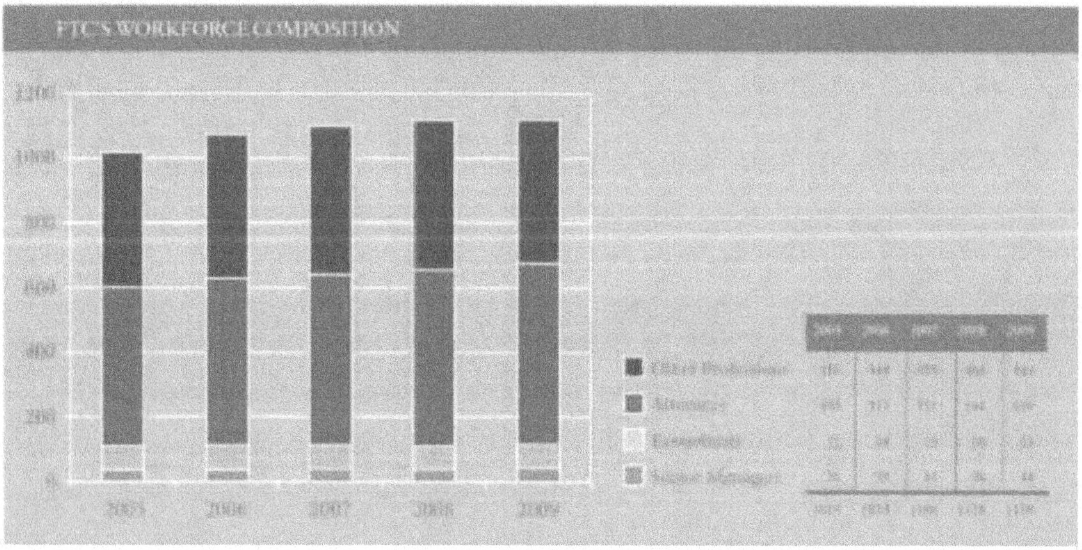

NASA

The National Air and Space Administration's (NASA) MD&A contains a concise and graphic mission/organization section as follows.

Our Mission

Congress enacted the National Aeronautics and Space Act of 1958 to provide for research into problems of flight within and outside the Earth's atmosphere and to ensure that the United States conducts activities in space devoted to peaceful purposes for the benefit of mankind. Our mission is:

To pioneer the future in space exploration, scientific discovery and aeronautics research.

NASA's Organization

NASA is comprised of its Headquarters in Washington, D.C., nine Centers located around the country, and the Jet Propulsion Laboratory, a Federally Funded Research and Development Center operated under a contract with the California Institute of Technology. In addition, we have partnership agreements with academia, the private sector, state and local governments, other Federal agencies, and a number of international organizations, creating an extended NASA family of civil servants, contractors, allied partners, and stakeholders.

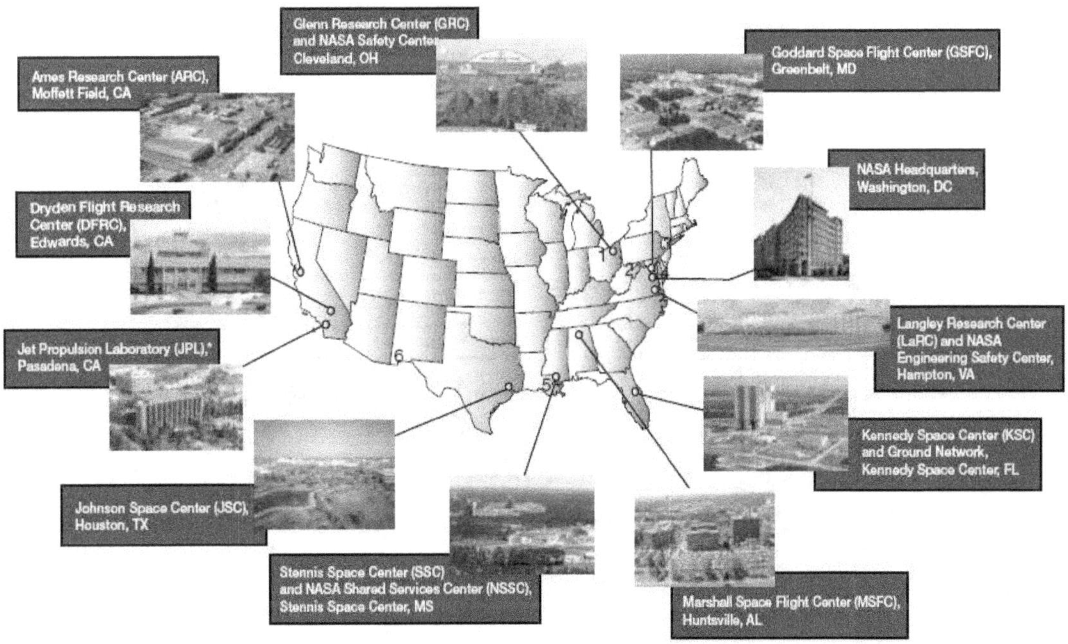

NASA's science, research, and technology development work is conceived of and implemented through its four Mission Directorates:

The **Aeronautics Research Mission Directorate (ARMD)** conducts fundamental research in aeronautical disciplines and develops capabilities, tools, and technologies that will significantly enhance aircraft performance, safety, and environmental compatibility, as well as increase the capacity and flexibility of the U.S. air transportation system.

The **Science Mission Directorate (SMD)** conducts the scientific exploration of Earth, the Sun, the solar system, and the universe. Missions include ground-, air-, and space-based observatories, deep-space automated spacecraft, and planetary orbiters, landers, and surface rovers. SMD also develops innovative science instruments and techniques in pursuit of NASA's science goals.

The **Exploration Systems Mission Directorate (ESMD)** develops the capabilities for long-duration human and robotic exploration. In support of the near-term goal of lunar exploration, ESMD is conducting robotic precursor missions, developing human transportation elements, creating innovative life support and medical technologies, and establishing international and commercial partnerships.

The **Space Operations Mission Directorate (SOMD)** directs spaceflight operations, space launches, and space communications and manages the operation of integrated systems in low Earth orbit and beyond, including the International Space Station (ISS). SOMD is laying the foundation for future missions to the Moon and Mars by using the ISS as an orbital outpost where astronauts can test systems and technology.

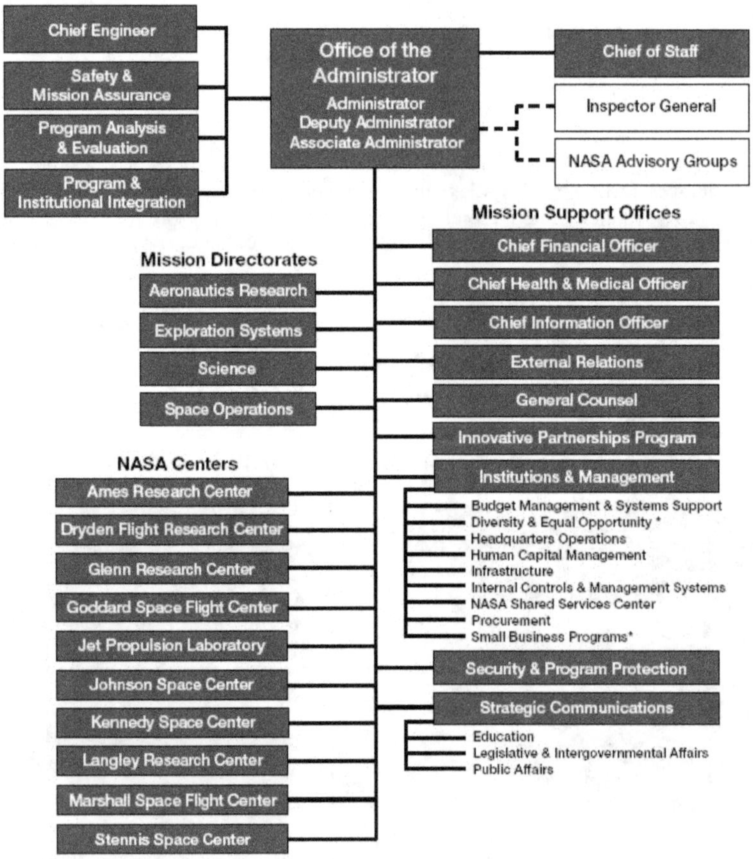

NASA organization as of September 30, 2009.

NASA's Mission Support Offices ensure that critical support functions for facilities, resources (human, financial, material), and institutional systems are ready and available to maximize the success of the research, technology development, and operational missions. For more detailed information about the functions represented in the NASA organization go to *www.nasa.gov/about/org_index.html*.

NASA's Workforce

NASA employs over 18,000 civil servants at our nine Centers, Headquarters, and the NASA Shared Services Center, with an additional 5,000 people at the Jet Propulsion Laboratory. We have employees at facilities in 12 states and Washington, D.C. Having NASA employees spread out across the country means that much of the general U.S. public is close to a NASA Center or facility, and has the ability to develop a personal connection to NASA.

As we enter the second decade of the 21st century, there is a greater diversity of age in our workforce than ever before, with four generations working side by side in many of our organizations. Currently NASA is implementing new programs to pull more Generation Y workers, those with birth dates starting from the mid-1970s, into the NASA community as a way to strengthen our diversity and skill sets. New employees will be able to learn from expert employees, retaining valuable institutional knowledge that would otherwise be lost to future generations. The Office of Human Capital Management is implementing a new program called the Early-Career Hiring Initiative to increase the number of people hired for entry-level and early-career positions.

NASA remains one of the best places to work in the Federal government ranking third in the Partnership for Public Service's 2009 Best Places to Work survey of Federal agencies as identified by employees (see *data.bestplaces-towork.org/bptw/index* for more information). We ranked particularly high in strategic management, teamwork, leadership, and support of diversity. This ranking is a 2.8 percent improvement over the last survey, conducted in 2007. We are proud to provide this level of employee satisfaction and are committed to improving our ranking in the future.

Shared Values, Shared Results

NASA has four shared core values that support our commitment to technical excellence and express the ethics that guide our behavior. Every NASA employee believes that mission success is the natural outcome of an uncompromising commitment to safety, technical excellence, teamwork, and integrity.

Safety: Constant attention to safety is the cornerstone upon which we build mission success. We are committed, individually and as a team, to protecting the safety and health of the public, NASA team members, and the assets that the Nation entrusts to the Agency.

Integrity: We are committed to maintaining an environment of trust, built upon honesty, ethical behavior, respect, and candor. Our leaders enable this environment by encouraging and rewarding a vigorous, open flow of communication on all issues, in all directions, and among all employees without fear of reprisal. Building trust through ethical conduct as individuals and as an organization is a necessary component of mission success.

Teamwork: We strive to ensure that our workforce functions safely at the highest levels of physical and mental well-being. The most powerful tool for achieving mission success is a multi-disciplinary team of diverse, competent people across all NASA Centers. Our approach to teamwork is based on a philosophy that each team member brings unique experience and important expertise to project issues. Recognition of and openness to the insight of individual team members improves the likelihood of identifying and resolving challenges to safety and mission success. We are committed to creating an environment that fosters teamwork and processes that support equal opportunity, collaboration, continuous learning, and openness to innovation and new ideas.

Excellence: To achieve the highest standards in engineering, research, operations, and management in support of mission success, we are committed to nurturing an organizational culture in which individuals make full use of their time, talent, and opportunities to pursue excellence in both the ordinary and the extraordinary.

Budgeting for Performance: NASA's FY 2009 Budget

NASA's Fiscal Year (FY) 2009 budgetary resources totaled $17,782 million, an increase of about 2.2 percent from NASA's FY 2008 Budget. This increase demonstrates a commitment to funding the balanced priorities set forth for the Agency in space exploration, Earth and space science, and aeronautics research.

NASA's FY 2009 Enacted Budget Total: $17,782
(Dollars in Millions)

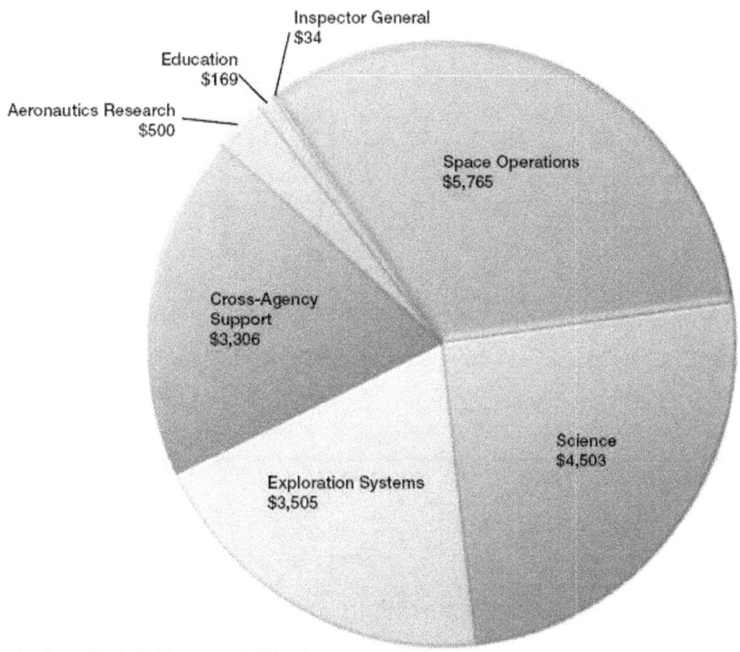

Note: Amounts do not include Recovery Act funds.

Proud to Serve the Nation: American Recovery and Reinvestment Act

The American Recovery and Reinvestment Act of 2009 (Recovery Act) was signed into law by President Obama on February 17, 2009. It is an unprecedented effort to jumpstart our economy, create and save millions of jobs, and modernize our Nation's infrastructure so our country can thrive in the 21st century.

We received $1,002 million in Recovery Act funds. Details on our progress are available at *www.nasa.gov/recovery/index.html*. From satellites that track and trend weather and natural hazards to creating a safer, more efficient air transportation system, our employees are proud to contribute to the breakthroughs and activities that will aid America's economic recovery.

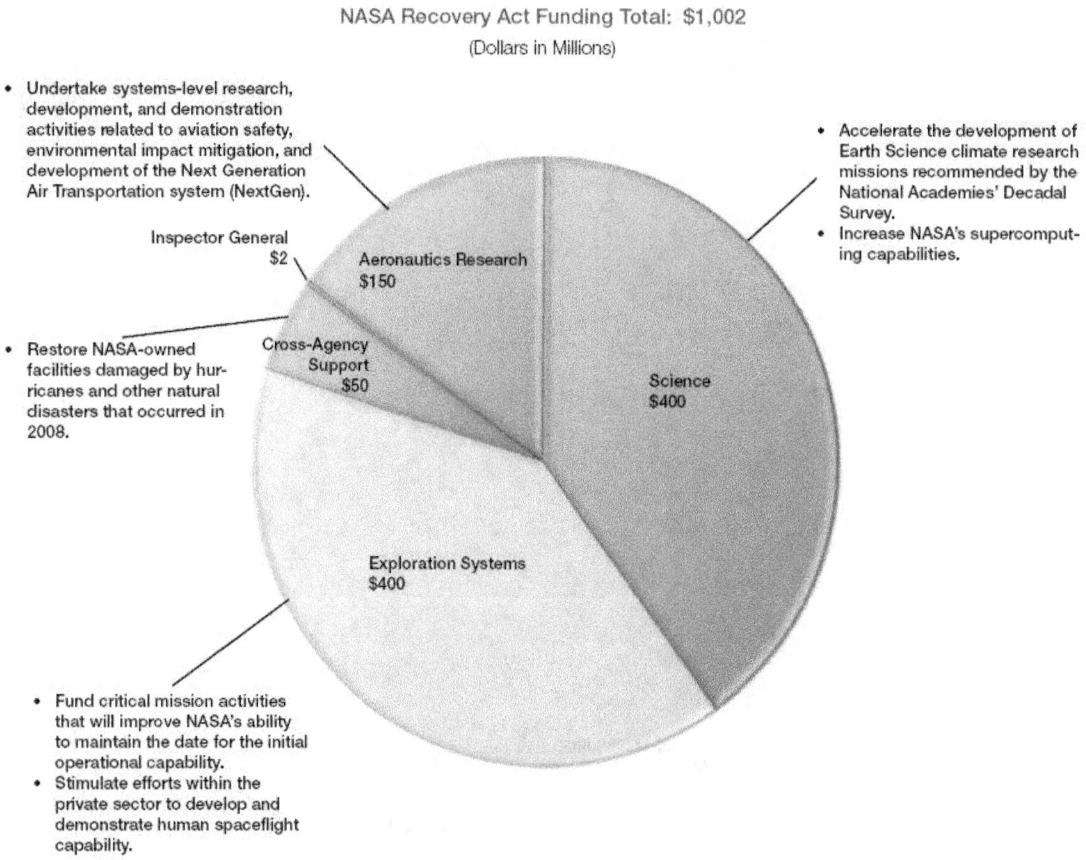
NASA Recovery Act Funding Total: $1,002
(Dollars in Millions)
• Undertake systems-level research, development, and demonstration activities related to aviation safety, environmental impact mitigation, and development of the Next Generation Air Transportation system (NextGen).
Inspector General $2
Aeronautics Research $150
• Restore NASA-owned facilities damaged by hurricanes and other natural disasters that occurred in 2008.
Cross-Agency Support $50
Science $400
Exploration Systems $400
• Accelerate the development of Earth Science climate research missions recommended by the National Academies' Decadal Survey.
• Increase NASA's supercomputing capabilities.
• Fund critical mission activities that will improve NASA's ability to maintain the date for the initial operational capability.
• Stimulate efforts within the private sector to develop and demonstrate human spaceflight capability.

Patent and Trademark Office

The Patent and Trademark Office's (PTO) MD&A provides an excellent example for presenting a great deal of information about "mission and organizational structure" in a table as follows.

2007-2012 USPTO Strategic Plan

Mission

To foster innovation and competitiveness by:

- Providing high quality and timely examination of patent and trademark applications
- Guiding domestic and international intellectual property policy
- Delivering intellectual property information and education worldwide

Vision

USPTO: Leading the World in Intellectual Property Protection and Policy

Strategic Goal #1	Strategic Goal #2	Strategic Goal #3	Management Goal
Optimize Patent Quality and Timeliness	Optimize Trademark Quality and Timeliness	Improve Intellectual Property Protection and Enforcement Domestically and Abroad	Achieve Organizational Excellence
Objectives	**Objectives**	**Objectives**	**Objectives**
▪ Provide high quality examination of patent applications ▪ Improve and integrate existing electronic systems to promote full electronic patent application processing; implement better/more secure systems ▪ Improve the quality and timeliness of patent examination by exploring a range of approaches to examining applications	▪ Achieve and maintain three-month first action pendency, and reduce average total pendency excluding suspended and *inter partes* cases ▪ Improve quality of examination by ensuring consistency and quality of searching and examination, and provide internal on-line tools ▪ Provide electronic file management and workflow ▪ Develop interactive on-line electronic filing capabilities and upgrade e-tools	▪ Support efforts and initiatives aimed at strengthening IP protection and curbing theft of IP ▪ Continue efforts to develop unified standards for international IP practice ▪ Provide policy guidance on domestic IP issues ▪ Foster innovation and competitiveness by delivering IP information and education worldwide	▪ Function as true business partners across the organization to achieve superior enterprise performance and provide strategic leadership ▪ Ensure operational excellence in enterprise-wide management processes ▪ Dramatically simplify on-line access to, and availability of, USPTO information and data

Performance Measures by Goal

Goal #1 Measures	Goal #2 Measures	Goal #3 Measures
▪ Patent allowance compliance rate ▪ Patent in-process examination compliance rate ▪ Patent average first action pendency ▪ Patent average total pendency ▪ Patent applications filed electronically	▪ Trademark final compliance rate ▪ Trademark first action compliance rate ▪ Trademark average first action pendency ▪ Trademark average total pendency ▪ Trademark applications processed electronically	▪ Percentage of countries on the United States Trade Representative (USTR) 301 list, awaiting World Trade Organization (WTO) accession, or targeted by Office of Intellectual Property Policy and Enforcement (OIPPE) for improvements that have positively amended or improved their IP systems ▪ Number of countries that implement at least 75% of action steps which improve IP protections in the joint cooperation, action or work plans

PERFORMANCE GOALS, OBJECTIVES, AND RESULTS

The ***performance objectives, goals, and results*** section of the MD&A should highlight the key performance measures for a "vital few"[3] matters, programs, etc. and relate them to strategic goals. In deciding which matters to present, the entity should consider who the stakeholders are. The MD&A should focus on matters of substantial interest to external users (citizens, the public, etc.), and avoid matters that are primarily if not exclusively internal, such as routine internal management processes. External users often will neither understand nor care about such matters.

For the federal government, the distinction between "internal" and "external" users is more difficult to make than for states and local governments or the private sector where the primary audience for general purpose financial statements is investors and creditors. The Board has stated that, in general, users of federal financial information fall into the four categories identified in SFFAC 1: citizens, Congress, executives, and program managers. However, for information at the more highly summarized governmentwide or consolidated level, the Board divided the four groups identified in SFFAC 1 into two major groups: external users (citizens), and internal users (Congress, executives, and program managers).

Presenting concise performance information is a challenge. The tendency is to include a lot of information rather than applying a rigorous relevancy or "vital few" test.

Performance measures should relate costs to outputs and outcomes. Cost information should stimulate interest in determining where resources are going or will go. Any change in how a performance measure is calculated should be explained. Such changes can affect the outcome, including causing an agency to meet a goal they otherwise would have failed to meet (or vise-versa).

The large array of performance measures is daunting and not likely to be read and therefore has not been identified as a "best practice."

In addition, the "vital few" unmet performance goals should be discussed because the agency's target should be challenging.

Focusing on clear, measurable outcomes and goals contributes to effective government operations.[4] The MD&A is an opportunity for management to frankly and concisely explain the essentials of performance, and to go beyond the usual formulaic communication. The Government Performance and Results Act of 1994 (GPRA) and various administrations before and since 1994 have sought to focus on outcomes and create useful performance measures. However, OMB has noted that current GPRA-

---

[3] SFFAS 15, par. 6.

[4] See OMB's "high priority performance goals" ("HPPG) initiative as explained in the Analytical Perspectives section of the FY 2011 budget.

based performance goals and measures are not being used. Congress does not use them to conduct oversight, agencies do not use them to manage, and the public does not use them to evaluate government operations. Moreover, OMB has noted that past performance management efforts generally have been ineffective; they have identified problems involving management policy and planning rather than focusing on outcomes.

OMB states that current performance reports seldom answer the questions of key audiences. The OMB's recent "high priority performance goals (HPPG) initiative requires agencies to commit to a limited number of ambitious, realistic, and achievable high-priority goals to be achieved within 24 months without additional resources or legislation; it requires agencies to have a limited number (generally three to eight) of well-defined, outcome-based measures of performance.

The HPPG initiative contrasts with the typical MD&A discussion of performance in current reports. The latter often discusses very high level strategic goals and, when discussing operations, uses (1) general, usually positive statements and (2) a complex table of performance measures that may be challenging to understand.

The following presentation of MD&A performance sections includes some references to the HPPG initiative.

Commerce Department

Among the extensive material in its discussion of performance in the FY 2009 MD&A, the Commerce Department presents an effective chart relating organizational structure (bureaus) to the three strategic objectives as follows.

DEPARTMENTAL PERFORMANCE STRUCTURE

The Department focuses on three different, yet inter-related aspects of economic growth and opportunity—growth, innovation, and environment—with each aspect reflected in each of the Department's strategic goals. A fourth goal—management integration—is linked to all three goals, focusing on various aspects of improving the management of the Department. The Department has 13 bureaus, each of which appears in a specific strategic (or management integration) goal, the lone exception being the National Institute of Standards and Technology (NIST) which appears in both Strategic Goals 1 and 2. This structure and the descriptions of each goal and corresponding objectives appear below.

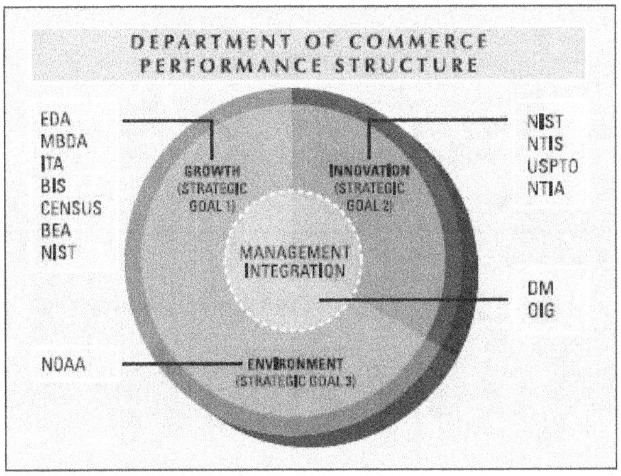

The Department promotes growth by developing partnerships with state, local, private, and non-profit enterprise so as to encourage economic growth and development (objective 1.1). The Department also encourages trade by promoting U.S. exports (objective 1.1) while at the same time monitoring those exports to prevent any export of goods that could be used for any activities against the United States (objective 1.2). The Department also develops and publishes economic statistics and indicators (e.g., gross domestic product [GDP]) essential to U.S. business (objective 1.3). Finally, the Department promotes the growth and competitiveness of the Nation's manufacturing industry (objective 1.4).

Defense Department

Defense Department's MD&A provides a concise and easily understood description of DoD's key performance outcomes as they relate to their strategic goals.

Program Performance Overview

DEPARTMENT OF DEFENSE STRATEGIC PLAN

The Department examines America's defense needs by conducting the Quadrennial Defense Review (QDR) to provide a blueprint for a strategy-based, balanced, and affordable defense program. The Department is conducting the QDR for FY 2010 as required by law and it will be completed and released by February 1, 2010. The QDR 2010 will tie to the new National Security Objectives and establish the Administration's approach to carrying out defense objectives. As required for the AFR, the remainder of this section discusses the performance plan and goals for FY 2009. These goals were based on the QDR 2006 and will be updated when QDR 2010 is complete. A copy of the Department's QDR 2006 can be found at www.defenselink.mil/qdr/report/Report20060203.pdf.

Figure 1-6

FY 2009 Strategic Goals
Goal 1
Successfully Conduct Overseas Contingency Operations
Goal 2
Reorient Capabilities and Forces
Goal 3
Reshape the Defense Enterprise
Goals 3 & 4 are Supporting Goals
Goal 4
Develop a 21st Century Total Force
Goal 5
Achieve Unity of Effort

The QDR 2006 was the first contemporary defense review to coincide with an ongoing major conflict. Consequently, Strategic Goal 1 (Figure 1-6) focuses on the ongoing major conflict and extended stabilization campaigns in Iraq and Afghanistan. At the same time, QDR 2006 recognized that the Department needed to recast its view of future warfare through the lens of a long duration and globally distributed conflict. Therefore, Strategic Goal 2 focuses on reorienting the Armed Forces to deter and defend against transnational terrorists around the world. Strategic Goal 5 recognizes that DoD cannot meet today's complex challenges alone. This goal recognizes integrated security cooperation and strategic communication as additional tool sets the Combatant Commanders may use to fight wars. Together, these three goals encompass the Department's warfighting missions. Strategic Goals 3 and 4 focus on reshaping the defense infrastructure and developing a Total Force, respectively, in ways that better support the warfighter. These supporting goals enable accomplishment of the Department's primary Strategic Goals 1, 2, and 5.

[5]

[5] AFR – Agency Financial Report.

DEPARTMENT OF DEFENSE PERFORMANCE BUDGET HIERARCHY

Figure 1-7 depicts the Department's performance budget hierarchy. This hierarchy highlights that every level within the Department is accountable for measuring performance and delivering results at multiple tiers of the organization.

Primary responsibility for performance improvement in DoD rests with the Deputy Secretary of Defense in his role as the Chief Management Officer (CMO). The Deputy Secretary is assisted by a Deputy CMO and the DoD Performance Improvement Officer (PIO), who advises and integrates performance information across DoD. The DoD strategic objectives and performance targets are recommended by Principal Staff Assistants (PSAs) within the Office of the Secretary of Defense, in coordination with the Joint Staff, as most relevant for enterprise or DoD-wide strategic focus. The DoD strategic objectives and performance targets (measures and milestones) are subject to annual refinement based on changes in missions and priorities.

Department of Defense Agency Financial Report for FY 2009

FISCAL YEAR 2009 DEPARTMENT OF DEFENSE KEY PERFORMANCE OUTCOMES

The Department submitted its detailed Fiscal Year (FY) 2009 Performance Plan in the FY 2009 Budget Request Summary Justification dated February 4, 2008 that is available at http://www.defenselink.mil/comptroller/defbudget/fy2009/FY2009_Budget_Request_Justification.pdf. This initial plan included 51 performance targets at the enterprise, or DoD-wide level.

Since that time, the Deputy Secretary of Defense/CMO approved some changes to this initial plan that resulted in a net reduction of two in the number of enterprise-level performance targets (from 51 to 49) for FY 2009. The following tables, organized by QDR Strategic Goal and Strategic Objective, depict 16 key performance outcomes for FY 2009. Based on fourth quarter data, the Department met or showed improvement in 88 percent (Figure 1-8) of these key outcome areas when compared to prior year (FY 2008) results.

Strategic Goal 1: Successfully Conduct Overseas Contingency Operations

Since 2001, the Department has been engaged in developing the forces and capabilities of Iraq and Afghanistan to provide for their own defense. Iraqi Security Forces (ISF) training is critical to enabling the Department to reallocate its resources and military forces in FY 2010 and beyond to Afghanistan and other regions as may be directed. Consequently, two key outcomes under this goal area focus on training Iraqi and Afghan Security forces as primary indicators for transitioning the security of both nations to their respective governments. By the end of FY 2009, the Department significantly surpassed its annual performance target with regard to training Iraqi Security Forces and accomplished 98 percent of its performance goal associated with the number of trained/assigned Afghan National Security Forces (ANSF).

Figure 1-7

Figure 1-8

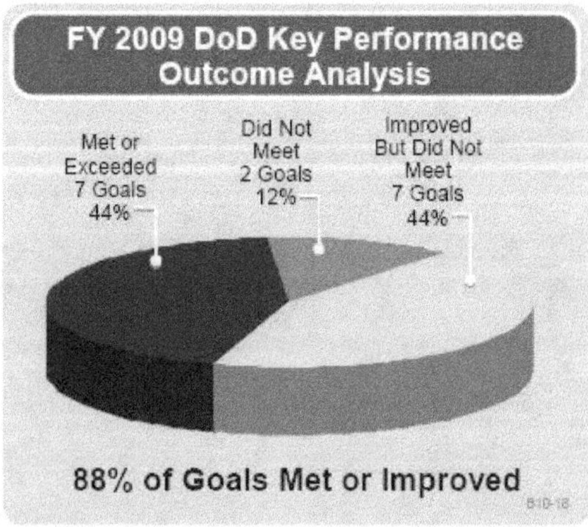

Department of Defense Agency Financial Report for FY 2009

STRATEGIC GOAL 1 (revised): SUCCESSFULLY CONDUCT OVERSEAS CONTINGENCY OPERATIONS				
Performance Measures	**Strategic Plan Long-term Performance Targets**	**Annual Performance Targets/Results**		
		FY 2008 Results	FY 2009 Targets	FY 2009 Results
Strategic Objective 1.1:	**Conduct a large-scale, potentially long-duration irregular warfare campaign that includes counterinsurgency, security stability, transition, and reconstruction operations.**			
1.1-1a: Cumulative number of ISF trained	1.1-1a: By FY 2009, the DoD will train 588,000 ISF	558,279	588,000	Sensitive[1]
1.1-1b: Cumulative number of ANSF trained/assigned	1.1-1b: By FY 2009, the DoD will develop a trained/assigned ANSF level of 187,196.	144,000	187,196	184,059

1/ DoD previously reported on the number of Iraqi Security Forces personnel authorized and assigned by the Ministries of Defense and Interior and trained with the assistance of Coalition forces. With the expiration of the mandate of UNSCR 1790, the data is now considered sensitive as it pertains to the specific military personnel strength for a sovereign nation.

Strategic Goal 2: Reorient Capabilities and Forces

Five key performance outcomes relate to the Department's second goal to reorient its capabilities and forces. The first two outcomes reflect new DoD capabilities necessary to mitigate attacks on the U.S. and its territories. A third measure focuses on increasing DoD Special Operations Forces capabilities to address irregular/unconventional warfare. The final two outcomes are focused on converting Army force structure to modular designs required to meet military operational missions and achieving significant transformation of the Army in a generation.

STRATEGIC GOAL 2: REORIENT CAPABILITIES AND FORCES				
Performance Measures	**Strategic Plan Long-term Performance Targets**	**Annual Performance Targets/Results**		
		FY 2008 Results	FY 2009 Targets	FY 2009 Results
Strategic Objective 2.1 (Revised): Improve capabilities to prevent and mitigate attacks on U.S. personnel, facilities, and key assets.				
2.1-1: Number of National Guard Weapons of Mass Destruction –Civil Support Teams (WMD-CSTs) certified	2.1-1: By FY 2009, 55 National Guard WMD-CSTs will be certified.	53	55	55
2.1-2: Number of National Guard CBRNE Enhanced Response Force Packages (CERFPs) trained	2.1-2: By FY 2008, 17 National Guard CERFPs will be trained for WMD or other catastrophic responses.	17	17	15

Department of Defense Agency Financial Report for FY 2009

STRATEGIC GOAL 2: REORIENT CAPABILITIES AND FORCES				
Performance Measures	Strategic Plan Long-term Performance Targets	Annual Performance Targets/Results		
		FY 2008 Results	FY 2009 Targets	FY 2009 Results
Strategic Objective 2.2:	**Deter and defend against transnational terrorists attacks and globally distributed aggressors and shape the choices of countries at strategic crossroads, while postured for a second, nearly simultaneous campaign.**			
2.2-2: Percent increase in DoD Special Forces and Navy SEAL personnel achieved	2.2-2: By FY 2012, the DoD will increase its Special Forces and Navy SEAL personnel by 32 percent from the FY 2006 actual of 13,206 end strength.	12.4%	17%	23%
2.2-4a: Number of Army Brigades Combat Teams (BCTs) converted to a modular design and available to meet military operational demands.	2.2-4a: By FY 2013, 76 modular Army BCTs will be available to meet military operational demands.	38	47	46
2.2-4b: Number of Army Multi-functional and Functional (MFF) Support brigades converted to a modular design and available to meet military operational demands.	2.2-4b: By FY 2013, 227 modular Army MFF brigades will be available to meet military operational demands.	188	201	196

Strategic Goal 3: Reshape the Defense Enterprise

Three key performance outcomes are identified as representative samples of the Department's enterprise reshaping goal. The first outcome, average customer wait time, is used by DoD's logistics community to improve joint warfighting support for maintenance and repair activities of major equipment and sustainment of the operating forces. Two other key outcomes focus on improving the quality of life for Service Members and their families. The strategic goals optimize long-term performance, readiness, and return on investment of facilities across the Department. These measure the number of inadequate military housing units in the continental U.S. (CONUS) and outside the continental U.S. (OCONUS).

STRATEGIC GOAL 3: RESHAPE THE DEFENSE ENTERPRISE				
Performance Measures	Strategic Plan Long-term Performance Targets	Annual Performance Targets/Results		
		FY 2008 Results	FY 2009 Targets	FY 2009 Results
Strategic Objective 3.3:	**Implement improved logistics operations to support joint warfighting priorities.**			
3.3-1: Average customer wait time (days)	3.3-1: Beginning in FY 2007, DoD will reduce average customer wait time to 15 days.	16.7	15	16.2

Department of Defense Agency Financial Report for FY 2009

STRATEGIC GOAL 3: RESHAPE THE DEFENSE ENTERPRISE				
Performance Measures	**Strategic Plan Long-term Performance Targets**	**Annual Performance Targets/Results**		
		FY 2008 Results	FY 2009 Targets	FY 2009 Results
Strategic Objective 3-4:	**Maintain capable, efficient, and cost-effective installations to support the DoD workforce.**			
3.4-4a: Number of inadequate family housing units CONUS	3.4-4b: By FY 2009, DoD will eliminate all inadequate family housing CONUS	5,085	0	4,600
3.4-4b: Number of inadequate family housing units OCONUS	3.4-4b: By FY 2009, DoD will eliminate all inadequate family housing OCONUS	7,273	0	2,367

Strategic Goal 4: Develop a 21st Century Total Force

Four key performance outcomes under this goal are focused on sustaining the capacity of the All-Volunteer Force to meet DoD steady-state and surge activities. Two measures assess DoD Active and Reserve component end-strength against levels prescribed by the Secretary of Defense for mission accomplishment. A third measures the percent of Armed Forces without any deployment-limiting medical conditions to ensure readiness for mission capability. A fourth, and final key outcome, under this goal, is focused on closing the current gap in language capabilities by assessing the percent of operational and contingency language skills to meet mission requirements.

STRATEGIC GOAL 4: DEVELOP A 21ST CENTURY TOTAL FORCE				
Performance Measures	**Strategic Plan Long-term Performance Targets**	**Annual Performance Targets/Results**		
		FY 2008 Results	FY 2009 Targets	FY 2009 Results
Strategic Objective 4.1:	**Ensure an "All Volunteer" military force is available to meet the steady-state and surge activities of the DoD.**			
4.1-1a: Percent variance in Active component end strength.	4.1-1a: For each fiscal year, the DoD Active component end strength will not vary by more than three percent from the SECDEF prescribed end strength for that fiscal year.	2.1%	+/- 3%	0.9%
4.1-1b: Percent variance in Reserve component end strength.	4.1-1b: For each fiscal year, the DoD Reserve component end strength will not vary by more than three percent from the SECDEF prescribed end strength for that fiscal year.	0%	+/-3%	1%

Department of Defense Agency Financial Report for FY 2009

STRATEGIC GOAL 4: DEVELOP A 21ST CENTURY TOTAL FORCE				
Performance Measures	Strategic Plan Long-term Performance Targets	Annual Performance Targets/Results		
		FY 2008 Results	FY 2009 Targets	FY 2009 Results
Strategic Objective 4.1:	**Ensure an "All Volunteer" military force is available to meet the steady-state and surge activities of the DoD.**			
4.1-2: Percent of deployable Armed Forces without any deployment- limiting medical condition.	4.1-2: By FY 2010, DoD will sustain the percent of deployable Armed Forces without any deployment-limiting medical condition to equal to or greater than 92 percent.	84%	>92%	85%
Strategic Objective 4.4:	**Improve workforce skills to meet mission requirements.**			
4.4-1: Percent of operational and contingency language needs met	4.4-1: By FY 2011, DoD will increase the percent of operational and contingency language needs met by three percent from the FY 2008 baseline.	Non-applicable	+1%	<.1%

Strategic Goal 5: Achieve Unity of Effort

The Department's fifth and final strategic goal focuses on building the capacity of international partners by improving access to equipment, technology, and training. Two key outcomes involve risk-reduction activities to control export of technology and activities that shape the international environment toward U.S. interest and track training capabilities among international partners for countering threats and challenges of terrorism. The first outcome focuses on increasing the number of international students participating in DoD-sponsored educational activities. The second measures the number of various technological and security reviews of goods and services approved for transfer to international partners.

STRATEGIC GOAL 5: ACHIEVE UNITY OF EFFORT				
Performance Measures	Strategic Plan Long-term Performance Targets	Annual Performance Targets/Results		
		FY 2008 Results	FY 2009 Targets	FY 2009 Results
Strategic Objective 5.1:	**Build capacity of international partners in fighting the war on terror.**			
5.1-1: Annual number of international students participating in Department-sponsored educational activities	5.1-1: Beginning in FY 2007, the DoD will increase the number of international students participating in Department-sponsored educational activities by at least two percent per year.	55,895	56,400	60,409
5.1-2: Annual number of Technology Security Actions (TSAs) approved	5.1-2: Beginning in FY 2007, DoD will increase the number of relevant technologies involving transfers to international partners by two percent per year.	118,367	120,704	143,600

Final year-end results for all 49 DoD performance outcomes will be addressed in the Department's more detailed performance report for FY 2009, submitted with the DoD's FY 2011 Congressional Budget Justification, on or about February 1, 2010. This report will be posted with the FY 2011 budget materials at http://www.defenselink.mil/comptroller/.

Environmental Protection Agency

The Environmental Protection Agency's (EPA) effective MD&A performance data includes a very informative U.S. map color coded by EPA region reporting an accomplishment for each EPA region as follows.

Highlights of Environmental

Region 8 EPA Protects At-Risk Communities

Based on health risks documented by Region 8's remedial investigation, investigations conducted by the Agency for Toxic Substances and Disease Registry, and concerns expressed by the community and state political leaders, in June 2009 EPA determined that a public health emergency exists at the Libby Asbestos Superfund Site in Northwest Montana. This marked the first EPA determination under the Comprehensive Environmental Response, Compensation and Liability Act that conditions at a site constitute a public health emergency. The unprecedented determination underscored the need for further action and health care for area residents who have been or may be exposed to asbestos. As a result, the U.S. Department of Health and Human Services awarded a grant to provide medical care to the residents of Lincoln County, while EPA continued its expeditious elimination of human exposure pathways at the site. http://www.epa.gov/region8/superfund/libby/index.html

Region 10 EPA Reports on Toxics in the Columbia River Basin

In 2009, EPA released the first *Columbia River Basin State of the River Report for Toxics*, a compilation of data about four widespread contaminants in the basin and the risks they pose to people, fish, and wildlife. The Region led a team of more than 20 partner organizations to draw this latest portrait of the toxic threats in the Columbia Basin, which drains nearly 260,000 square miles across seven states. http://yosemite.epa.gov/r10/ecocomm.nsf/Columbia/Columbia

Region 9 The American Reinvestment and Recovery Act (ARRA) Saves Jobs

At the Iron Mountain Mine Superfund site, EPA has spent $20.7 million in ARRA funds, which will reduce cleanup time from three years to 18 months. Work completed will enable the removal of 170,000 cubic yards of contaminated sediments from the bottom of Keswick Reservoir downstream from the mine and eliminate a major threat to the Sacramento River ecosystem, the most important salmon spawning grounds in California. Federal hydropower facilities will be able to generate $3 million to $6 million worth of additional peak power each year. The project has created or saved more than 200 jobs. www.epa.gov/region09/ironmountainmine

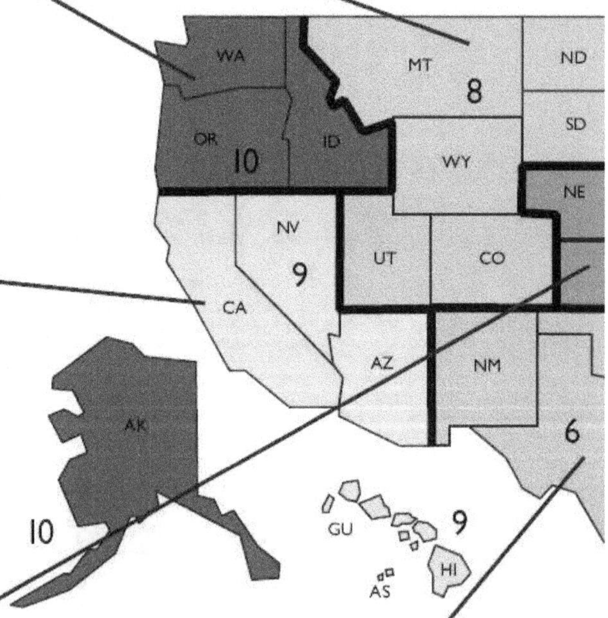

Region 7 Conducts Massive Lead Clean-up

Through September 15, 2009, EPA Region 7 has cleaned up lead-contaminated soil from 1,128 residential properties at eight Superfund lead/mining sites in Missouri and Nebraska. Specifically, lead contamination has been removed from 807 properties within the Omaha lead site, and the remaining 321 cleanups occurred at sites in southeastern and southwestern Missouri. Region 7's use of site-specific contracts on these sites has enabled the Region to meet 100 percent of its small business goals. In FY 2009, Region 7 awarded all Superfund-American Reinvestment and Recovery Act funding to small businesses. http://www.epa.gov/region07/cleanup/npl_files/index.htm

Region 6 BP Consent Decree Will Control Pollution

A settlement with BP Products North America Inc. resulted in the company paying a penalty of $12 million for violations of the Clean Air Act regulations. The settlement also requires BP to spend more than $161 million on pollution controls and enhanced maintenance and monitoring, and $6 million on a supplemental project to reduce air pollution in Texas City. EPA estimates that these actions will reduce emissions of benzene and other volatile organic compounds by approximately 6,000 pounds annually, providing a substantial benefit to the 4,700 people living less than 1 mile from the refinery. http://www.epa.gov/compliance/resources/cases/civil/caa/bptexas.html

Accomplishment, EPA Regions

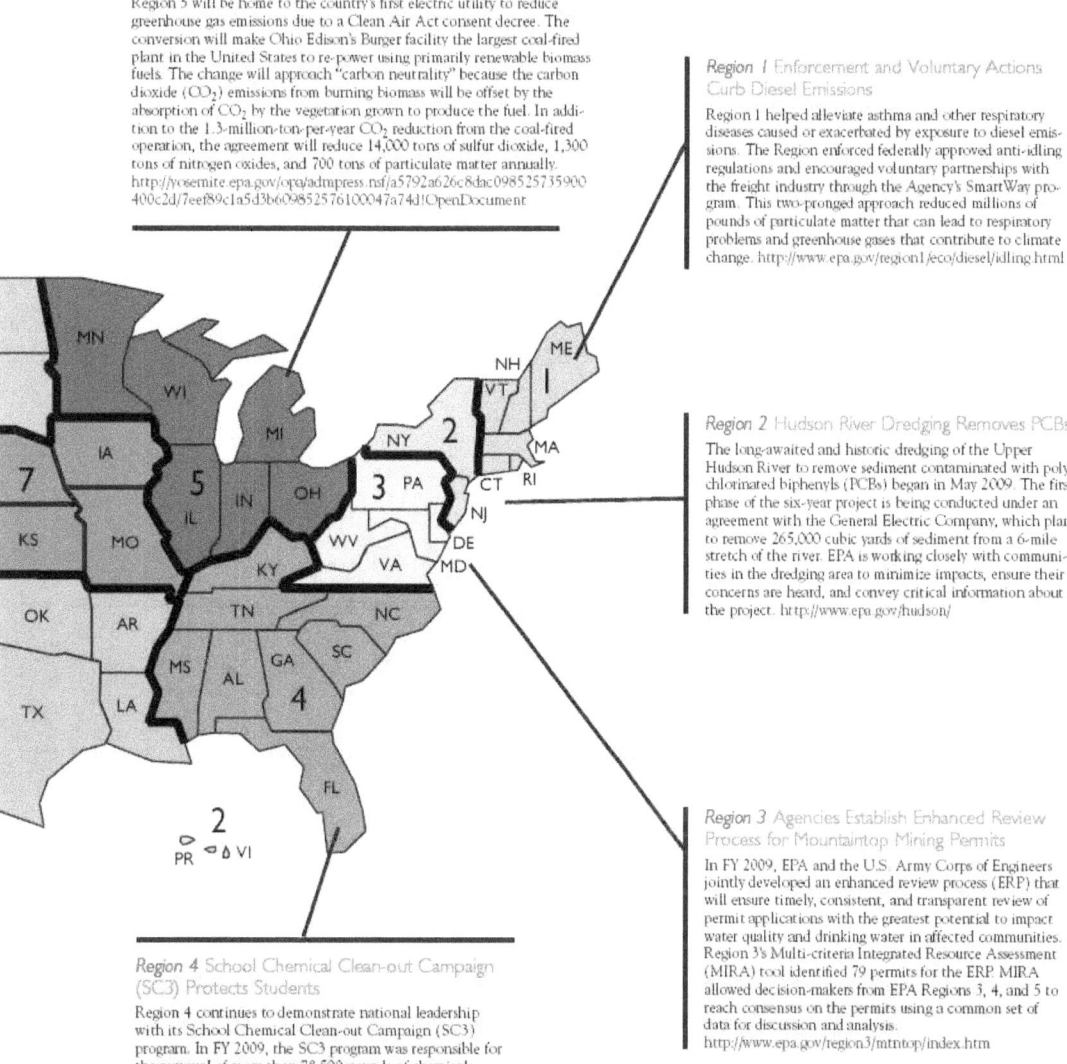

Region 5 A Coal-Fired Plant Re-Powers With Renewable Biomass Fuel

Region 5 will be home to the country's first electric utility to reduce greenhouse gas emissions due to a Clean Air Act consent decree. The conversion will make Ohio Edison's Burger facility the largest coal-fired plant in the United States to re-power using primarily renewable biomass fuels. The change will approach "carbon neutrality" because the carbon dioxide (CO_2) emissions from burning biomass will be offset by the absorption of CO_2 by the vegetation grown to produce the fuel. In addition to the 1.3-million-ton-per-year CO_2 reduction from the coal-fired operation, the agreement will reduce 14,000 tons of sulfur dioxide, 1,300 tons of nitrogen oxides, and 700 tons of particulate matter annually. http://yosemite.epa.gov/opa/admpress.nsf/a5792a626c8dac098525735900400c2d/7eef89c1a5d3b6098525761000 47a74d!OpenDocument

Region 1 Enforcement and Voluntary Actions Curb Diesel Emissions

Region 1 helped alleviate asthma and other respiratory diseases caused or exacerbated by exposure to diesel emissions. The Region enforced federally approved anti-idling regulations and encouraged voluntary partnerships with the freight industry through the Agency's SmartWay program. This two-pronged approach reduced millions of pounds of particulate matter that can lead to respiratory problems and greenhouse gases that contribute to climate change. http://www.epa.gov/region1/eco/diesel/idling.html

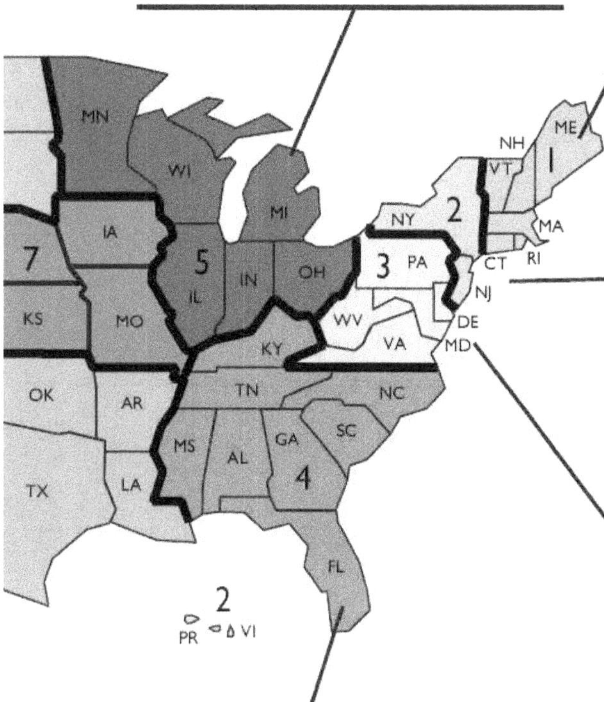

Region 2 Hudson River Dredging Removes PCBs

The long-awaited and historic dredging of the Upper Hudson River to remove sediment contaminated with polychlorinated biphenyls (PCBs) began in May 2009. The first phase of the six-year project is being conducted under an agreement with the General Electric Company, which plans to remove 265,000 cubic yards of sediment from a 6-mile stretch of the river. EPA is working closely with communities in the dredging area to minimize impacts, ensure their concerns are heard, and convey critical information about the project. http://www.epa.gov/hudson/

Region 3 Agencies Establish Enhanced Review Process for Mountaintop Mining Permits

In FY 2009, EPA and the U.S. Army Corps of Engineers jointly developed an enhanced review process (ERP) that will ensure timely, consistent, and transparent review of permit applications with the greatest potential to impact water quality and drinking water in affected communities. Region 3's Multi-criteria Integrated Resource Assessment (MIRA) tool identified 79 permits for the ERP. MIRA allowed decision-makers from EPA Regions 3, 4, and 5 to reach consensus on the permits using a common set of data for discussion and analysis.
http://www.epa.gov/region3/mtntop/index.htm

Region 4 School Chemical Clean-out Campaign (SC3) Protects Students

Region 4 continues to demonstrate national leadership with its School Chemical Clean-out Campaign (SC3) program. In FY 2009, the SC3 program was responsible for the removal of more than 78,500 pounds of chemicals (including 180 pounds of mercury) from 110 schools, impacting over 53,400 students.
http://www.epa.gov/region4/waste/rcra/sc3.htm

The EPA mentions the total number of its performance measures (205) but it does not try to present them in the MD&A. For example, no long textual passages or daunting table are presented. The EPA presents percentages for met, unmet, and data not available, and presents a discussion of "key accomplishments" and "challenges by Objective and Strategic Goal" in a "highlights of program performance by goal" (see pages 13-35). Although 22 pages of discussion seem excessive, the EPA presents it effectively.

Federal Aviation Administration

The Federal Aviation Administration's (FAA) MD&A is effective. It presents 31 performance measures for four strategic goals with minimal narrative using an informative table as follows.

PERFORMANCE HIGHLIGHTS

The FAA is charged with promoting the safety and efficiency of the Nation's aviation system. With broad authority to enforce safety regulations and conduct oversight of the civil aviation industry, we maintain the system's integrity and reliability. A strategic plan, annual business plans, human capital plans, and the annual PAR create a recurring cycle of planning, program execution, measurement, verification, and reporting. This strong link between resources and performance shows our accomplishments and reinforces accountability for the way we spend taxpayer money.

Managing Performance

The FAA manages performance by using a four-step framework based on best practices from a number of private and public sector organizations (See chart below).

PERFORMANCE MANAGEMENT FRAMEWORK

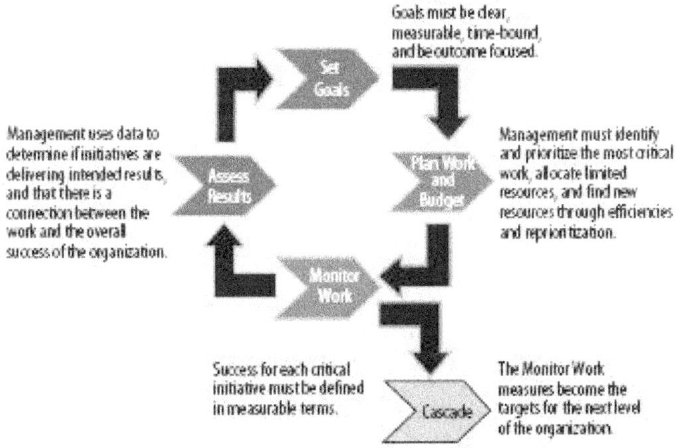

As we use this framework and instill management discipline into the processes, we anticipate a multiyear journey of learning and change.

YEAR-TO-YEAR PERFORMANCE GOALS ACHIEVED							
	FY 2003	FY 2004	FY 2005	FY 2006	FY 2007	FY 2008	FY 2009
Performance Targets Met (Number)	9 of 12	24 of 30	28 of 31	27 of 30	24 of 30	26 of 29	28 of 31
Performance Targets Met (Percentage)	75%	80%	90%	90%	80%	90%	90%

The first step in the process, Set Goals, includes consulting with management, stakeholders, and customers to identify areas for improvement.

The second step, Plan Work and Budget, focuses on the critical work and resources required to achieve the goals. Following the framework, the FAA created a performance-based budget that links resource requirements to the *Flight Plan* and the DOT Strategic Plan. Our FY 2009 Budget in Brief is available at http://www.faa.gov/about/budget and our *Flight Plan* is available at http://www.faa.gov/about/plans_reports.

The third step, Monitor Work, develops measurement of the work required to achieve our goals. The FAA has developed organizational business plans for each LOB and staff office. These plans outline the initiatives, activities, and performance targets that link our work directly to the *Flight Plan*. FY 2009 Business Plans for all organizations are available at http://www.faa.gov/about/plans_reports.

The *Flight Plan*, the FAA's strategic plan, consists of 31 strategic performance measures in FY 2009. It is carefully designed to make sure that we focus on what is important, and that taxpayer resources are used with the strictest care. The *Flight Plan* measures are categorized into four strategic goal areas—Increased Safety, Greater Capacity, International Leadership, and Organizational Excellence. When setting the goals, the agency strives to increase the challenge each year.

Assess Results is the last and most important step in the performance management process. This year, we continued our practice of reviewing and discussing annual performance goals every month. In addition, we continued to focus more on discussing performance results, root causes of performance issues, and reallocation of resources to correct underperformance.

Our performance measures and targets support the FAA's mission to provide citizens with a safe, secure, and efficient global aviation system. The chart above provides a summary of our year-to-year performance goal achievement trend.

As indicated in the chart above, the FAA has expanded its strategic focus since 2002. As we continue to mature in our strategic management processes and our focus becomes sharper, the number and mix of performance targets shift. On a yearly basis, we review the plan to ensure that we are on track to meet future challenges and to ensure that aviation remains an engine of economic growth.

When we first started preparing our annual PAR in FY 2002, the FAA had 10 performance goals in the strategic areas of Safety, System Efficiency, and Organizational Excellence. In 2003, the FAA refined its strategic plan and launched the first *Flight Plan* (FY 2004–2008). The *Flight Plan* provides the framework to match resources with initiatives for long-term change. The new *Flight Plan* was designed around our current four strategic goals. These goals detail how we will move forward into the future.

In FY 2004, to reflect the increasing emphasis on accountability within the FAA organizations, we added 18 new performance targets. Six of the new performance targets were associated with International Leadership and placed greater emphasis on our role as a leader in the global civil aviation system. In the Safety strategic goal area, we introduced Commercial Space Launch Accidents, marking a new era in space travel, with FAA licensing of the first private manned space vehicle—SpaceShipOne.

In FY 2009—the sixth year of the *Flight Plan's* implementation—the FAA has 31 performance measures and targets that focus our efforts to achieve enhanced aviation safety, increase system capacity, provide international leadership, and ensure organizational success. We met 28—a 90 percent success rate.

GSA

The General Services Administration's (GSA) MD&A and financial report as a whole is fully Web-based. GSA presents several key performance measures for each GSA strategic goal. There are menu selections for "GSA Overview", Key Performance Measures", "Financial Results", and Assurances and Management Challenges". GSA's report is available on the Web at the address listed in Table 1 above.

Justice Department

The Justice Department's FY 2009 MD&A performance section is concise and informative. A table with the 25 "key performance measures" is presented under the menu selection for "analysis of performance information" (see the Web address in Table 1) and is well done, as shown in part immediately below:

[ ] Designates the reporting entity	FY 2009 Target	FY 2009 Actual	Target Achieved/ Not Achieved
Strategic Goal I: Prevent Terrorism and Promote the Nation's Security			
Terrorist acts committed by foreign nationals against U.S. interests within U.S. borders **[FBI]**	Zero	Zero	Achieved
Catastrophic acts of domestic terrorism **[FBI]**	Zero	Zero	Achieved
Strategic Goal II: Prevent Crime, Enforce Federal Laws, and Represent the Rights and Interests of the American People			
Number of organized criminal enterprises dismantled **[FBI]**	36	39	Achieved
NEW MEASURE: Number of children depicted in child pornography rescued by the FBI **[FBI]** [1]	150	118	Not Achieved[2]
[1] This measure replaces the former measure: "Number of child pornography websites or web hosts shut down" due to an OMB-led program review in the Spring of 2008. [2] The FBI has not met its target for this measure. While the FBI always makes every effort to identify/rescue victimized children, the FBI cannot directly control the number of children identified and/or rescued at any given time through investigative techniques, due to the reactive nature of this measure.			
Percentage of firearms investigations resulting in a referral for criminal prosecutions **[ATF]**	59%	59%	Achieved
DOJ's reduction in the supply of illegal drugs available for consumption in the U.S. **[ADAG/Drugs]**	Progress toward establishing baseline[3]	N/A	TBD
[3] Measuring the reduction in the illegal drug supply is a complex process reflective of a number of factors outside the control of drug enforcement. Moreover, the impact of enforcement efforts on the illegal drug supply and the estimated availability are currently not measurable in a single year. However, the Department is intent on achieving an interim goal of setting a baseline by the close of FY 2010. Once the baseline is set, the Department intends to achieve a 6 percent total reduction in the supply of illegal drugs available for consumption in the United States over the next two years.			

Thus, the Justice Department presents goals that are generally fairly specific and consistent with the Justice Department's five "high priority performance goals" identified during the OMB performance initiative and published in the *Analytical Perspectives* of the FY 2009 Budget, page 82-83. These goals are described as a "subset of those used to regularly monitor and report performance", and are specific and generally quantified, e.g., "White Collar Crime: Increase white collar caseload by five percent concerning mortgage fraud, health care fraud, and official corruption b 2012, with 90 percent of cases favorably resolved." Fewer measures are a best practice in part because they can be easily tracked.

Department of Veterans Affairs

The Department of Veterans Affairs' (VA) Web-based MD&A provides a hyperlink to a summary performance table that provides a great deal of information about strategic goals, performance measures and results, as mentioned in a prior section of this report.

The table in combination with the performance overview (see immediately below) communicate this information effectively.

How We Measure Performance

VA employs a **five-tiered performance management framework** to measure performance.

Term	*Definition*
Strategic Goals	The Department's long-term outcomes as detailed in its Strategic Plan and articulated through four strategic goals and one enabling goal.
Strategic Objectives	Broad operational focus areas designed to achieve strategic goals. The Department has 21 strategic objectives.
Performance Measures	Specific measurable indicators used to measure progress towards achievement of strategic objectives. The Department uses different types of measures (i.e., outcome, output, and efficiency) to evaluate its performance and progress.
Performance Targets	Associated with specific performance measures, these are quantifiable expressions of desired performance/success levels to be achieved during a given fiscal year.
Strategic Targets	Also associated with specific performance measures, these are quantifiable expressions of optimum success levels to be achieved; they are "*stretch goals*" that VA strives for in the long-term.

VA's 21 strategic objectives are supported by 104 performance measures, 26 of which were identified by VA's senior leadership as **mission critical**. The Department's performance measures are a mix of program outcomes that measure the impact that VA programs have on the lives of Veterans and their families, program outputs that measure activities undertaken to manage and administer these programs, and program efficiency that measures the cost of delivering an output or desired outcome.

Key Features of the FY 2009 Report

VA's PAR includes several features designed to give our stakeholders more complete information on VA's performance and activities.

Key Feature	*Benefit to VA's Stakeholders*
Cost Per Measure Data	The Department is furthering its integration of performance and budget information. As part of this effort, this year's PAR includes information on the cost of achieving performance targets for ***nine*** measures. We provide this in addition to cost estimates provided by strategic goal and objective, respectively.
Major Management Challenges	This year's report improves how major management challenges are presented. VA's response to each challenge is presented in an easy-to-read tabular format providing an estimated resolution date, a responsible official, a summary of actions taken, milestones planned for FY 2010, and anticipated impacts of actions planned. In addition, the presentation now divides the response into three categories: People, Process, and Policy. Together these elements provide a comprehensive analysis of the challenges facing the Department and what VA is doing to address them.
Web Links	This year's PAR lists more VA Web links compared to last year's PAR.
Data Quality Information	This year's report contains more robust and detailed information on how VA verifies the quality of its performance results data. The report's Key Measures Data Table and the Assessment of Data Quality sections have been restructured to provide more comprehensive data quality information.
Dashboard Style Tables	Selected tables now include more dashboard-like features that convey performance results using easy-to-read tables and "traffic light" color coding to help the reader more quickly and clearly assess VA performance results.
VA Snapshots	Snapshots are short vignettes that give the reader an easy way to understand VA through human interest stories.
Strategic Objective Measures Recap	Our strategic objective chapters in Part II now include a recap of all measures and associated results for a given objective including a statistical recap.

Federal Housing Finance Administration

The FHFA presents an effective "summary of performance" about their strategic goals, performance goals, and key performance indicators as follows.

Key Performance Indicators for FY 2009

Strategic Goal	Performance Goal	Key Performance Indicator
STRATEGIC GOAL 1 Enhance supervision to ensure that Fannie Mae, Freddie Mac, and the Federal Home Loan Banks operate in a safe and sound manner, are adequately capitalized, and comply with legal requirements.	PERFORMANCE GOAL 1.1 **Fannie Mae and Freddie Mac (the Enterprises) comply with safety and soundness standards.**	PERFORMANCE MEASURE 1.1.1 The percentage of Enterprises with a composite GSE enterprise risk safety and soundness rating of "Limited Concerns" or better. **Not Achieved** Both Enterprises were rated "Critical Concerns" and were in conservatorship.
		PERFORMANCE MEASURE 1.1.2 For both Enterprises, the percentage of GSE enterprise risk categories (governance, solvency, earnings, market, credit, and operational risk) with a safety and soundness rating of "Limited Concerns" or better (1 or 2). **Not Achieved** Ratings for the Enterprises were "Critical Concerns" for earnings, credit risk, and market risk and "Significant Concerns" for governance and operational risk. In conservatorship, the rating for capital was suspended.
	PERFORMANCE GOAL 1. **The FHLBanks comply with safety and soundness standards.**	PERFORMANCE MEASURE 1.2.1 Percentage of FHLBanks with a composite rating of "1" or "2". **Not Achieved** Sixty-two percent of the FHLBanks (and the Office of Finance) had a composite safety and soundness rating of "1" or "2" at the end of the fiscal year. Heightened concerns about credit risk and governance associated with private-label MBS holdings contributed to the decline in ratings.
	PERFORMANCE GOAL 1.4 **The FHLBanks are adequately capitalized.**	PERFORMANCE MEASURE 1.4.1 The FHLBanks meet FHFA's determination of capital adequacy. **Substantially Achieved** FHLBanks met all capital requirements at year-end. One FHLBank, failed to meet the risk-based capital requirement for part of the year.

Strategic Goal	Performance Goal	Key Performance Indicator
STRATEGIC GOAL 1 Enhance supervision to ensure that Fannie Mae, Freddie Mac, and the Federal Home Loan Banks operate in a safe and sound manner, are adequately capitalized, and comply with legal requirements.	PERFORMANCE GOAL 1.5 **Fannie Mae and Freddie Mac comply with applicable laws, regulations, directives, and agreements, including executive compensation, corporate responsibility, and disclosure.**	PERFORMANCE MEASURE 1.5.1 Any identified instances of noncompliance with laws and regulations are resolved to FHFA's satisfaction. **Achieved** Enterprises resolved, or are on schedule to resolve, outstanding supervisory issues arising from laws, regulations, directives, and agreements.
	PERFORMANCE GOAL 1.6 **The FHLBanks comply with applicable laws, regulations, directives, and agreements, including those regarding executive compensation, cor-porate responsibility, and disclosure.**	PERFORMANCE MEASURE 1.6.3 Establish a matters requiring attention-like measure for tracking follow-up recommendations from annual exams. **Achieved** An MRA tracking tool was developed in 2009 and is being used for FHLBank examinations that commenced in 2009. Tracking tools for each FHLBank were backfilled with outstanding 2008 MRAs to log and document remediation efforts in a consistent manner.
STRATEGIC GOAL 2 Promote homeownership and affordable housing and support an efficient secondary mortgage market.	PERFORMANCE GOAL 2.1 **Develop proposed and final regulations to implement statutory changes in Fannie Mae and Freddie Mac affordable housing goals effective January 1, 2010, while enforcing existing goals.**	PERFORMANCE MEASURE 2.1.4 Enforce Fannie Mae and Freddie Mac 2009 affordable housing goals. **Achieved** Met monthly with each Enterprise to track progress in meeting housing goals.
	PERFORMANCE GOAL 2.2 **The FHLBanks foster the development of affordable owner-occupied and rental housing for eligible very low-, low-, and moderate-income households.**	PERFORMANCE MEASURE 2.2.2 The FHLBanks address principal affordable housing program examination findings to FHFA's satisfaction prior to the next examination. **Achieved** Conducted all scheduled affordable housing program exams and visitations, assessed status of principal affordable housing program examination findings from prior exam, and obtained management commitment to correct findings from 2009 examinations.

Strategic Goal	Performance Goal	Key Performance Indicator
STRATEGIC GOAL 2 Promote homeownership and affordable housing and support an efficient secondary mortgage market.	PERFORMANCE GOAL 2.5 Cooperate with other federal agencies on mortgage markets and the nation's housing finance system and regulatory issues.	PERFORMANCE MEASURE 2.5.1 Respond to requests from other Federal agencies for information about housing finance markets and the Enterprises. **Achieved** Thirty-day standard met on requests related to mortgage market conditions, debt issuance, Making Home Affordable, and Housing Finance Agency assistance.
STRATEGIC GOAL 3 Through conservatorship, FHFA will preserve and conserve the assets and property of Fannie Mae and Freddie Mac and enhance their ability to fulfill their mission.	PERFORMANCE GOAL 3.1 Preserve and conserve each Enterprise's assets and property.	PERFORMANCE MEASURE 3.1.1 Financial condition of each enterprise remains liquid and they maintain positive GAAP net worth including Senior Preferred Stock. **Achieved** The Treasury Preferred Stock Agreement continues to support the Enterprises positive net worth and sufficient capacity remains.
	PERFORMANCE GOAL 3.2 Continue to delegate appropriate authorities to each Enterprise's management to move forward with the business operations.	PERFORMANCE MEASURE 3.2.2 Establish new Boards of Directors at each Enterprise. **Achieved** Both Enterprises reconstituted their Boards of Directors in December, 2008.
RESOURCE MANAGEMENT STRATEGY Manage effectively FHFA's human capital and resources to support our mission.	PERFORMANCE GOAL 4.1 Maintain a diverse workforce that is skilled, flexible, and performance-oriented to fulfill the goals of the agency.	PERFORMANCE MEASURE 4.1.3 Percentage of vacancies filled within Office of Personnel Management's 45-day time-to-hire standard. **Achieved** FHFA met the 45-day time-to-hire standard in 73 percent of FY2009 hires.

ANALYSIS OF FINANCIAL STATEMENTS AND STEWARDSHIP INFORMATION SECTION

For the ***financial statement analysis*** section, the MD&A should focus on the changes in financial position and, thus, the results of operations during the period. It should relate financial results, performance, and costs to strategic goals. It should explain the significant variations from prior years, from the budget, and from performance plans. It should explain what happened and whether what happened is likely to continue in the future. Thus, the financial analysis should do more than merely describe the changes in financial statement line items that are obvious from the information on the face of the statements. In this regard, charts and tables are especially helpful.

Even if the financial statements have been read, often the true import of the data is not well understood by the reader. The MD&A should provide valuable information about financial results and trends that are not apparent from the face of the financials. The following are some examples of effective presentation of financial results.

Energy Department

In FY 2009, the Energy Department presented a bar graph on the first page of the financial statement analysis in the MD&A that shows total assets and liabilities (i.e., changes in financial position) since 2005, and a further breakdown by certain asset and liability types for 2009, as follows.

Total Assets and Liabilities with Breakdown of FY 2009 Liabilities

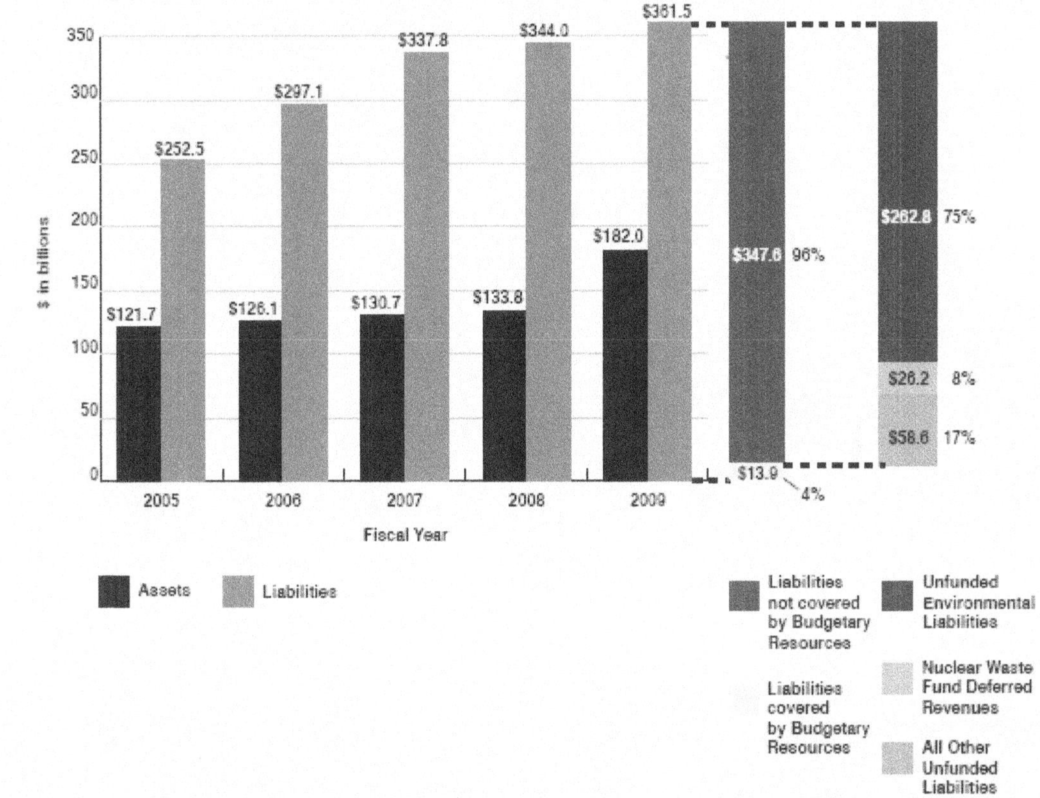

A further graphic decomposition of assets, liabilities and costs, with minimal narrative, is presented, as shown below.

Major Elements of Net Cost

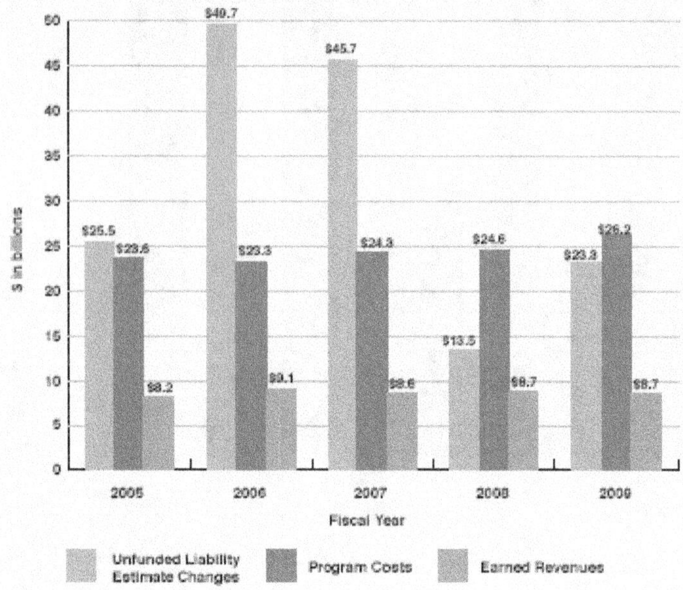

Composition of Environmental Cleanup and Disposal Liability

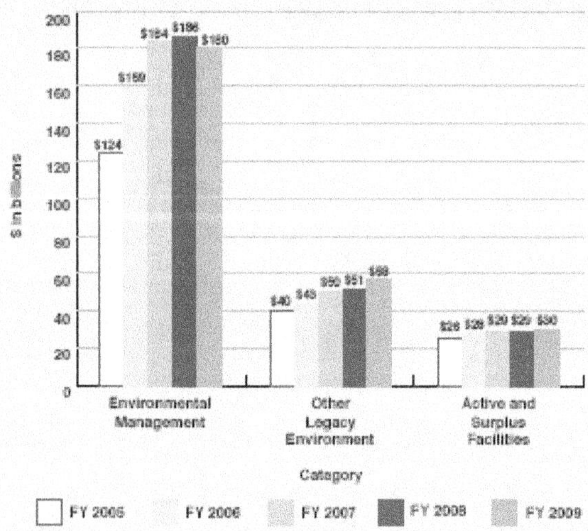

General Services Administration

As mentioned above, the General Services Administration's (GSA) financial report is fully Web-based. GSA presents a concise financial analysis for each strategic goal. See menu selection for "Financial Results" for the MD&A discussion at the Web site provided in Table 1 above.

Federal Aviation Administration

The Federal Aviation Administration (FAA) presents financial results using a good balance of narrative and graphs as follows.

FINANCIAL HIGHLIGHTS

Discussion and Analysis of the Financial Statements

The FAA prepares annual financial statements in conformity with accounting principles generally accepted in the United States. The financial statements are subject to an independent audit to ensure that they are free from material misstatement and that they can be used to assess FAA performance.

FY 2009 Financial Statement Audit

The CFO Act of 1990 (Public Law 101–576), as amended by the Government Management Reform Act of 1994, requires that financial statements be prepared by certain agencies and commercial-like activities of the Federal Government, and that the statements be audited in accordance with Government auditing standards. The FAA is required to prepare its own financial statements under OMB Bulletin No. 07–04, Audit Requirements for Federal Financial Statements. DOT's OIG is statutorily responsible for the manner in which the audit of the FAA's financial statements is conducted. The OIG selected Clifton Gunderson, LLP, an independent certified public accounting firm, to audit the FAA's FY 2009 financial statements.

In 2002, DOT's OIG and CFO, along with the FAA's CFO, established an Audit Coordination Committee to promote and encourage open communication among the OIG, FAA management, and the independent auditors to resolve issues that arise during the audit and to monitor the implementation of audit recommendations. The committee is chaired by the Director of the Office of Financial Management and includes representatives from the OIG, DOT's Office of Financial Management, FAA's Assistant Administrator for Regions and Center Operations, and ATO's Chief Operating Officer. In 2006, committee participation was expanded to include representatives from the Chief Counsel's Office, the Assistant Administrator for Human Resources Management, Information Services, and Airports.

Clifton Gunderson, LLP, has rendered an unqualified opinion on the FAA's FY 2009 financial statements.

Understanding the Financial Statements

The FAA's Consolidated Balance Sheets, Statements of Net Cost, Changes in Net Position, and Combined Statements of Budgetary Resources (beginning on page 96), have been prepared to report the financial position and results of operations of the FAA, pursuant to the requirements of the CFO Act of 1990 and the Government Management Reform Act of 1994. The following section provides a brief description of: (a) the nature of each financial statement and its relevance to the FAA; (b) significant fluctuations from FY 2008 to FY 2009; and (c) certain significant balances, where necessary, to help clarify their link to FAA operations.

Balance Sheet

The balance sheet presents the amounts available for use by the FAA (assets) against the amounts owed (liabilities) and amounts that comprise the difference (net position).

Assets

Total assets were $27.9 billion as of September 30, 2009. The FAA's assets are the resources available to pay liabilities or satisfy future service needs. The Composition of Assets chart depicts major categories of assets as a percentage of total assets. The Assets Comparison chart presents comparisons of major asset balances as of September 30, 2008 and 2009.

Fund Balance with Treasury represents 15 percent of the FAA's current period assets and consists of funding available through Department of Treasury accounts from which the FAA is authorized to make expenditures to pay liabilities. It also includes passenger ticket and other excise taxes deposited to the Airport and Airway Trust Fund (AATF), but not yet invested. Fund Balance with Treasury increased slightly from $3.9 billion to $4.1 billion.

At $9.2 billion, Investments represent 33 percent of the FAA's current period assets, and are principally derived from passenger ticket and other excise taxes deposited to

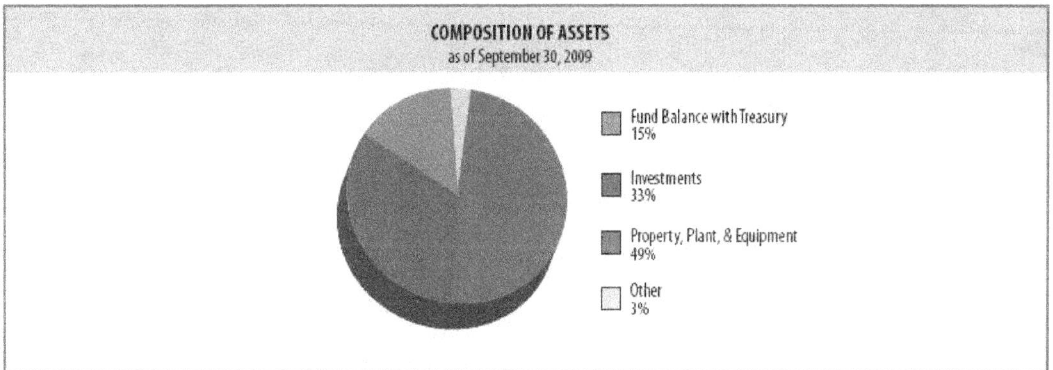

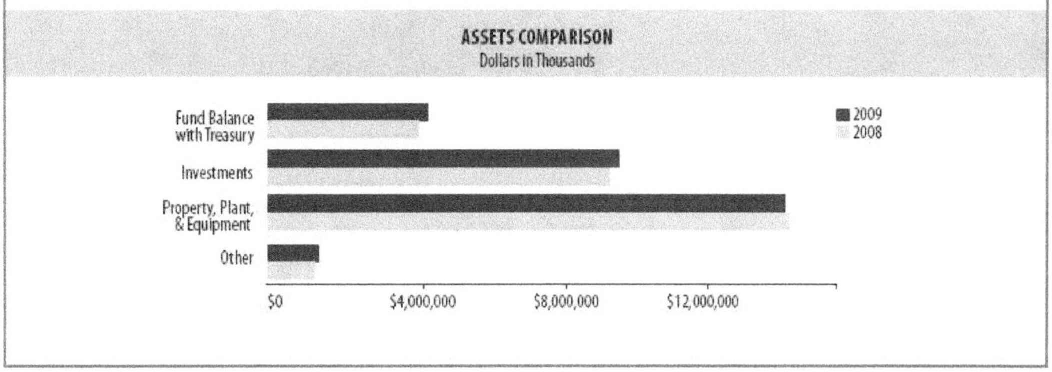

the AATF. These amounts are used to finance the FAA's operations to the extent authorized by Congress. Investments increased by $323.8 million.

At $13.8 billion, General Property, Plant, & Equipment represents 49 percent of the FAA's assets as of September 30, 2009, and primarily comprises construction-in-progress related to the development of NAS assets, and capitalized real and personal property. There was a slight decrease of $24.9 million in the total composition of Property, Plant, & Equipment as purchases of equipment and additions to construction-in-progress through the normal course of business were offset by retirements and depreciation.

Liabilities

As of September 30, 2009, the FAA reported liabilities of $4.4 billion. Liabilities are probable and measurable future outflows of resources arising from past transactions or events. The Composition of Liabilities chart depicts the FAA's major categories of liabilities as a percentage of total liabilities.

The Liabilities Comparison chart presents comparisons of major liability balances between September 30, 2008, and September 30, 2009. Below is a discussion of the major categories.

At $1.4 billion, Employee-Related & Other Liabilities represents 32 percent of the FAA's total liabilities. These liabilities increased slightly by $14.1 million as of September 30, 2009, and are composed mainly of $135.7 million in advances received, $211.0 million in Federal employees' compensation act payable, $337.2 million in accrued payroll and benefits, $481.5 million in accrued leave and benefits, $41.0 million in legal claims liability, and $115.8 million in capital lease liability.

At $901.3 million, Federal Employee Benefits represents 20 percent of the FAA's current year liabilities, and consists of the FAA's expected liability for death, disability, and medical costs for approved workers' compensation cases, plus a component for incurred but not reported claims. The Department of Labor calculates the liability for the DOT, and the DOT attributes a

COMPOSITION OF LIABILITIES
as of September 30, 2009

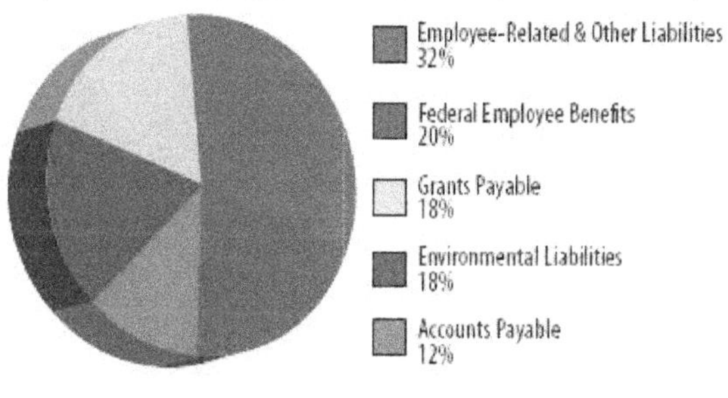

LIABILITIES COMPARISON
Dollars in Thousands

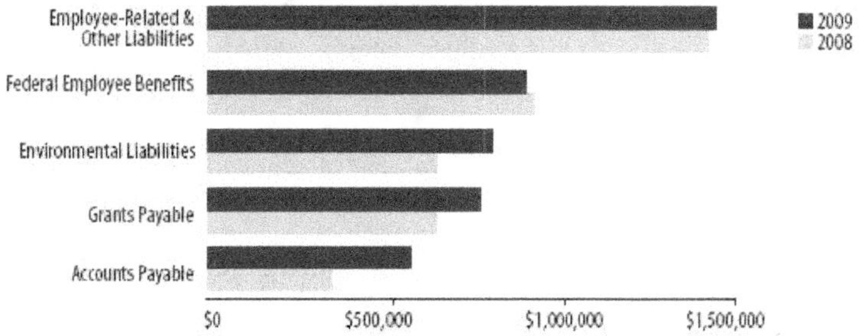

proportionate amount to the FAA based upon actual workers' compensation payments to FAA employees during the preceding 4 years. This liability is updated an on annual basis at year end.

Environmental Liabilities represents 18 percent of the FAA's total liabilities, $810.8 million as of September 30, 2009, compared with $637.8 million a year earlier. Environmental liabilities includes a component for remediation of known contaminated sites and the estimated environmental cost to decommission assets currently in service. The increase of $173.0 million is due primarily to an increase in the number of assets labeled "Areas of Concern," extending the time for onsite and program management by approximately 10 years.

The FAA's Grants Payable are estimated amounts incurred but not yet claimed by AIP grant recipients and represent 18 percent of liabilities. Grants payable increased $133.7 million primarily due to an accrual of $109.7 million for new grants awarded through the FY 2009 ARRA. Accounts Payable increased $173.9 million and are amounts the FAA owes to other entities for unpaid goods and services.

Statement of Net Cost

The Statement of Net Cost presents the cost of operating FAA programs. The gross expense less any earned revenue for each FAA program represents the net cost of specific program operations. The FAA has used its cost accounting system to prepare the annual Statement of Net Cost since FY 1999.

As of September 30, 2009, and September 30, 2008, the FAA's net costs were $16.4 billion and $15.5 billion, respectively. The Composition of Net Cost chart illustrates the distribution of costs among the FAA's LOBs.

The Net Cost Comparison chart compares September 30, 2008, and September 30, 2009, net costs.

With a net cost of $10.9 billion, the ATO is the FAA's largest LOB, composing 67 percent of total net costs. The ATO's net costs increased by $474.9 million, on a comparative basis, primarily from increases in labor costs of $190.0 million, and environmental cleanup and remediation of $173.0 million, which was partially offset

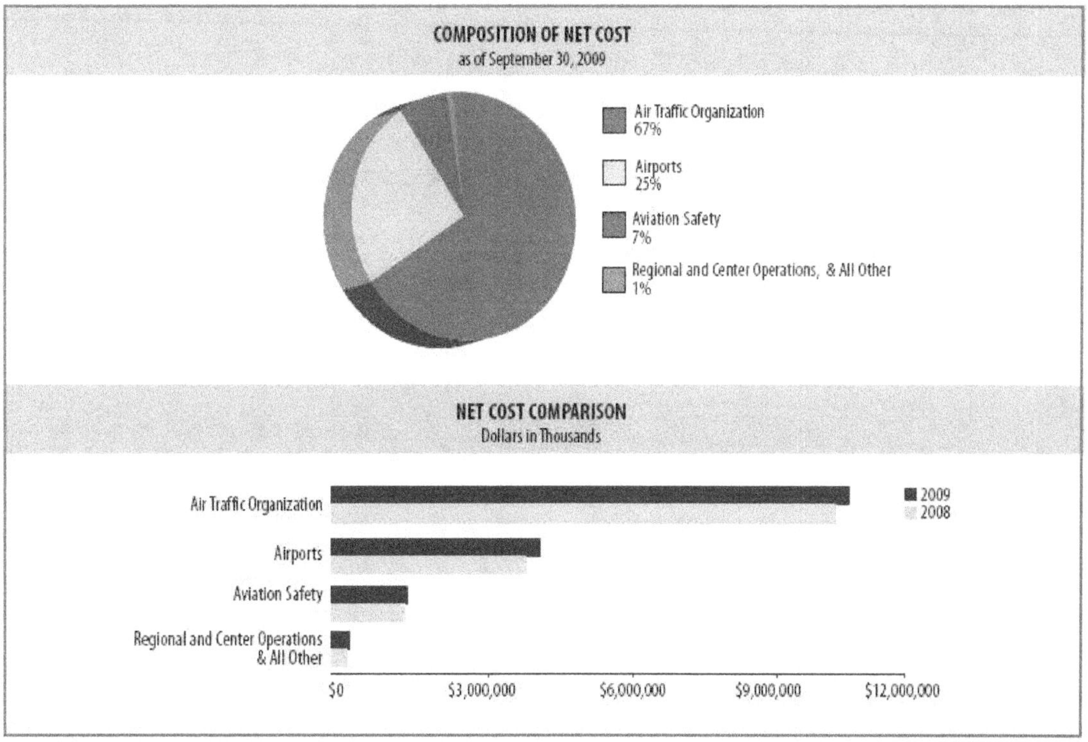

by an increase in reimbursable revenue from work in the NAS Defense Program of $62.0 million.

Airports is the FAA's second largest LOB with a net cost of $4.0 billion as of September 30, 2009, which is 25 percent of the FAA's total net costs. Net costs increased $280.9 million from the prior year and are composed mostly of Aviation Insurance Program grant disbursements.

The net cost of Aviation Safety represents 7 percent of the FAA's total net costs, while Regional and Center Operations and All Other compose 1 percent of total net costs.

Statement of Changes in Net Position

The Statement of Changes in Net Position presents those accounting items that caused the net position section of the balance sheet to change from the beginning to the end of the reporting period. Various financing sources increase net position. These financing sources include appropriations received and nonexchange revenue, such as excise taxes and imputed financing from costs absorbed on the FAA's behalf by other Federal agencies. The agency's net cost of operations and net transfers to other Federal agencies serve to reduce net position.

The FAA's cumulative results of operations for the period ending September 30, 2009, decreased $1.2 billion, on a comparative basis, due primarily to a combination of increases in net cost of $858.6 million and by decreases in beginning balances of $299.0 million and financing sources of $47.9 million. Unexpended appropriations increased $1.2 billion primarily as a result of an increase in appropriations received of $2.8 billion offset by an increase in appropriations used of $1.3 billion.

Statement of Budgetary Resources

This statement provides information on the budgetary resources available to the FAA as of September 30, 2009, and September 30, 2008, and the status of those budgetary resources.

Budget Authority is the authority provided to the FAA by law to enter into obligations that will result in outlays of Federal funds. Obligations Incurred results from an order placed, contract awarded, service received, or similar transaction, which will require payments during the same or a future period. Gross Outlays reflects the actual cash disbursed by Treasury for FAA obligations. The FAA reported total budget authority of $20.7 billion on September 30, 2009, compared to $19.5 billion on September 30, 2008. Obligations Incurred increased $391.5 million to $22.7 billion. Gross Outlays decreased $402.7 million from $22.0 billion to $21.6 billion.

Stewardship Investments

Stewardship investments are substantial investments made by the FAA for the benefit of the Nation, but do not result in physical ownership of assets by the FAA. When incurred, these amounts are treated as expenses in the Consolidated Statements of Net Cost. Our Required Supplementary Stewardship Information includes disclosure of stewardship investments during the last 5 years. These are disclosures of AIP grants by State/Territory, and research and development investments.

The distribution of total grants expense by State/Territory has been relatively stable during the past 4 years. However, expenses began to increase in FY 2005 largely as a result of a significant increase in grant

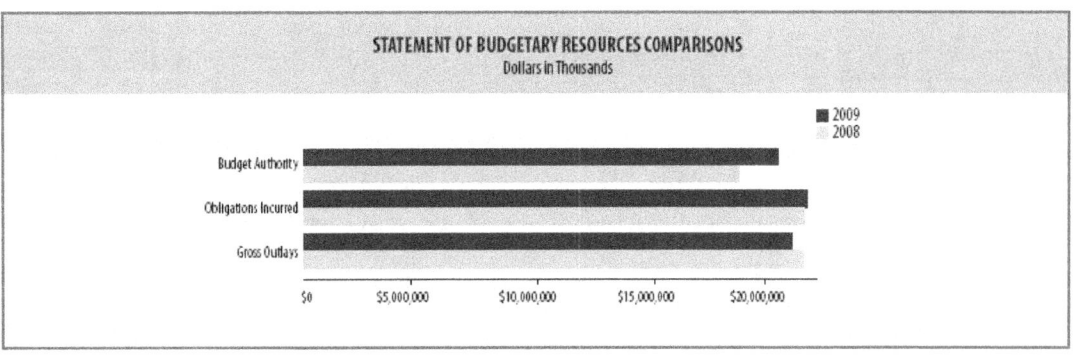

STATEMENT OF BUDGETARY RESOURCES COMPARISONS
Dollars in Thousands

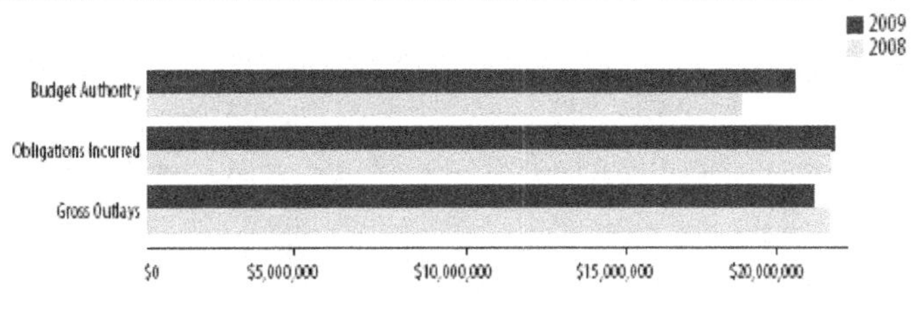

MANAGEMENT'S DISCUSSION AND ANALYSIS

funding levels in FY 2001. Because these AIP projects are typically long-term, and the FAA recognizes the grants expense as the recipient accomplishes the improvement work, the substantial expansion of this program in FY 2001 is resulting in increased expenses in more recent years.

The FAA's research and development expenses increased in FY 2009 by $9.4 million primarily in the category of applied research. Some areas of focus this year included the Commercial Aviation Alternative Fuel Initiative, developing enhanced weather forecasting models for quickly identifying hazardous ceiling and visibility conditions that impact air traffic capacity and the evaluation of replacing incandescent lamps for airfield lighting with light-emitting diodes to save on energy and maintenance costs.

Limitations of the Financial Statements

The FAA has prepared its financial statements to report its financial position and results of operations, pursuant to the requirements of the CFO Act of 1990 and the Government Management Reform Act of 1994.

While the FAA statements have been prepared from its books and records in accordance with the formats prescribed by the OMB, the statements are in addition to the financial reports used to monitor and control budgetary resources, which are prepared from the same books and records.

FAA ENACTED BUDGET--FY 2009
Dollars in Thousands

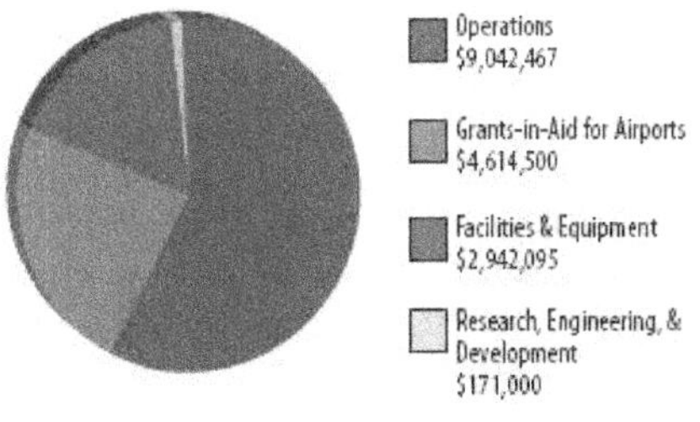

These statements should be read with the understanding that they are for a component of the U.S. Government, a sovereign entity. Liabilities not covered by budgetary resources cannot be liquidated without the enactment of an appropriation by Congress, and payment of all liabilities, other than for contracts, can be abrogated by the Federal Government.

Budgetary Integrity: FAA Resources and How They Are Used

In FY 2009, the AATF provided approximately 69.6 percent of the FAA's enacted budget. Created by the Airport and Airway Revenue Act of 1970, the AATF derives its funding from excise taxes and earned interest. It provides a source of revenue to finance investments in the airport and airway system. To the extent funds are available, the fund also covers the operating costs of the airway system. Aviation excise taxes, which include taxes on domestic passenger tickets, freight waybills, general and commercial aviation fuel, and international departures and arrivals, are deposited into the fund. The Department of the Treasury maintains the fund and invests in Government securities. Interest earned is deposited into the fund. Funding is withdrawn as needed and transferred into each FAA appropriation to cover obligations.

The FAA is funded through annual and multiyear appropriations authorized by Congress. The FY 2009 enacted budget of $16.77 billion was 12.4 percent higher than the FY 2008 enacted level. This includes $11.7 billion from the AATF and $5.1 billion from the General Fund. The Combined Statement of Budgetary Resources reflects $15.5 billion enacted by the Omnibus Appropriations Act of 2009 (PL 111-8) and $1.3 billion enacted from the ARRA (PL 111-5).

The FAA has four appropriations. The largest, Operations, is funded by both the Treasury's General Fund and the AATF. In FY 2009, the AATF provided 58 percent of the revenue for Operations. The AATF is the primary revenue source for the FAA's following three capital investment appropriations:

- Grants-in-Aid for Airports (AIP)
- F&E
- Research, Engineering, and Development (R,E,&D)

Small Business Administration

The FY 2009 Small Business Administration (SBA) annual report provides an example of management effectively explaining financial and operational results as shown below.

Results of Operations

The Results of Operations primarily reflects the costs of SBA credit programs from subsidy expenses during the year for new loans and subsidy reestimates at year end. The credit subsidy cost is the net present value of expected cash inflows and outflows over the life of a guarantied loan, or the difference between the net present value of expected cash flows and the face value of a direct loan. The SBA receives appropriations annually to fund its credit programs. When loans are disbursed, the SBA records subsidy expense. In accordance with the Federal Credit Reform Act, the subsidy costs are reestimated annually. Reestimates update original loan program cost estimates to reflect actual experience and changes in forecasts of future cash flows. Increased reestimated costs are funded in the following year by permanent indefinite authority, while decreased costs are returned by the SBA to a Treasury general fund. During FY 2009, the reestimated cost for the 7(a) and the 504 loan programs significantly increased (guarantied business loan program, Strategic Goal 1). Those increases were the largest components of the change (net increase) in the Agency's net cost. **Chart III** reflects the increases in the reestimates for the Disaster direct programs as well as the guarantied business loan program from FY 2008 to FY 2009.

CHART III

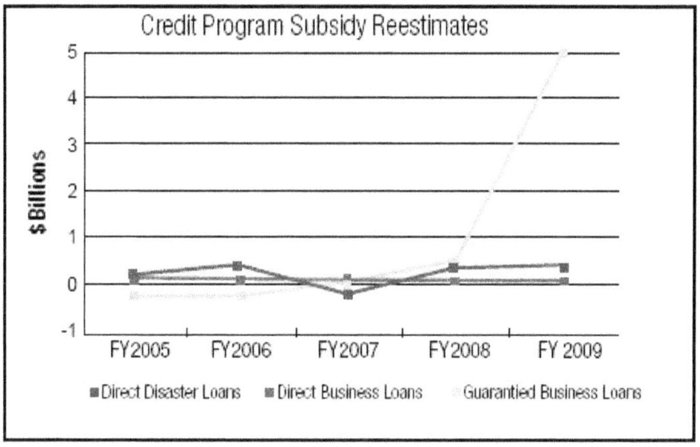

CHART IV

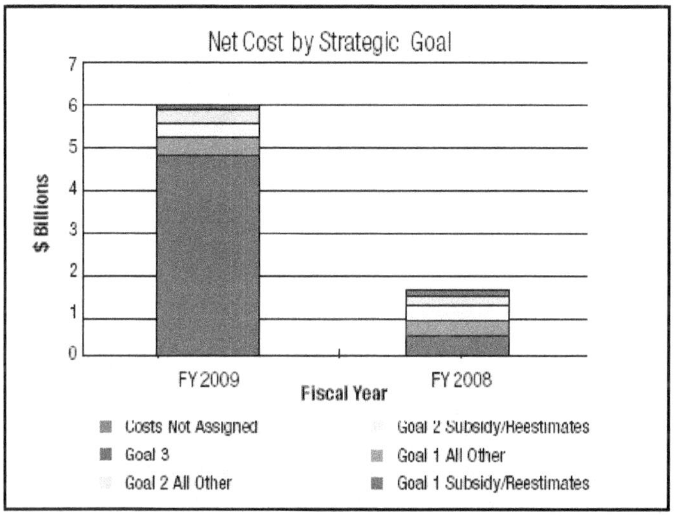

The increase in the overall Net Cost from FY 2008 to FY 2009 (see **Chart IV**) is primarily due to the increase in Strategic Goal 1 from the upward reestimates for the business loan guaranty programs in FY 2009. The 7(a) loan guaranty program and the 504 loan program both had significant upward reestimates as well as a significant change in the SBIC program from a downward reestimate in FY 2008 to an upward reestimate in FY 2009. The 7(a) loan program, SBA's flagship and largest program, had the largest net upward reestimates for the guarantied business loan programs in FY 2009 at $2.03 billion. The 504 Certified Development Companies program had net upward reestimates of $1.57 billion. For both programs, the net upward reestimates were mostly due to the downturn in the economy that resulted in higher than projected purchases during FY 2009 and an increase in projected purchases for the remaining years within the cohorts.

The SBIC debentures program had net upward reestimates of $66.6 million. The reestimates were mostly due to lower than projected recoveries during FY 2009 and a decrease in projected recoveries for the remaining years within the cohorts.

The SBIC participating securities program had a net upward reestimate of $960.2 million. The reestimates were mostly due to the downturn in the economy that resulted in lower than projected recoveries and higher than projected purchases during FY 2009 and an increase in projected purchases for the remaining years within the cohorts.

The secondary market guaranty program had a net downward reestimate of $50.8 million. This downward reestimate was due in part to the lower than projected interest rate paid to investors during FY 2009 and a decrease in the projected interest rate paid to investors for the remaining years within the cohorts.

The 7(a) and 504 Recovery Act programs had net upward reestimates of $72.4 million and $25.2 million respectively. These upward reestimates are mostly due to updated model and economic assumptions since the original budget estimates. The updated assumptions result in an increase in projected purchases for the remaining years within the cohorts.

There was also an increase in Strategic Goal 1 in subsidy expense incurred during FY 2009. This is due to the use of subsidy associated with the Recovery Act. The Recovery Act allocated $636 million of subsidy for loan guaranties. In FY 2008, there was no subsidy provided for the guarantied business loan programs. The reestimates, however, accounted for most of the change in Strategic Goal 1.

Strategic Goal 2 includes a net upward reestimate in the Disaster direct loan program at year end and an increase in administrative expenses during FY 2009 offset by a decrease in subsidy expenses. The Disaster program had net upward reestimates of $231.1 million primarily in the 2006 cohort that mostly consists of loans for the Gulf Coast hurricanes of 2005. Those loans currently account for about 55 percent of the outstanding portfolio of direct disaster loans. The upward reestimates are primarily the result of performance probabilities being updated with actual performance during FY 2009 that resulted in an increase in projected defaults.

Budgetary Resources

Total Budgetary Resources increased $3.2 billion from FY 2008 to FY 2009. This increase is reflected by increases in Borrowing Authority and Appropriations Received. Borrowing Authority increased by $2.1 billion in FY 2009 from FY 2008 as a result of borrowing to cover increases in purchases of defaulted loans. Purchases of SBA's share of defaulted guarantied loans increased from $2.1 billion to $3.9 billion from FY 2008 to FY 2009. Due to this unexpected surge in purchases, the SBA was required to borrow funds from Treasury to cover these purchases (see explanation for Debt with Treasury). Appropriations Received increased $1 billion from FY 2008 to FY 2009. The increase in Appropriations Received correlates with the increase in Unexpended Appropriations due to the funding in the Recovery Act legislation. In February 2009, as part of the stimulus package, Congress allocated $730 million for the SBA to provide new lending incentives including the Agency temporarily waiving its fees and increasing the guaranties it offers banks on 7(a) loans. **Chart V** depicts that the substantial increase in Appropriations Received is for business loans due to the Recovery Act. It also reflects the decrease in funding for disaster loans because, in September 2008, the Disaster Relief and Recovery Supplemental Appropriation Act had provided appropriations of $799 million for the SBA.

CHART V

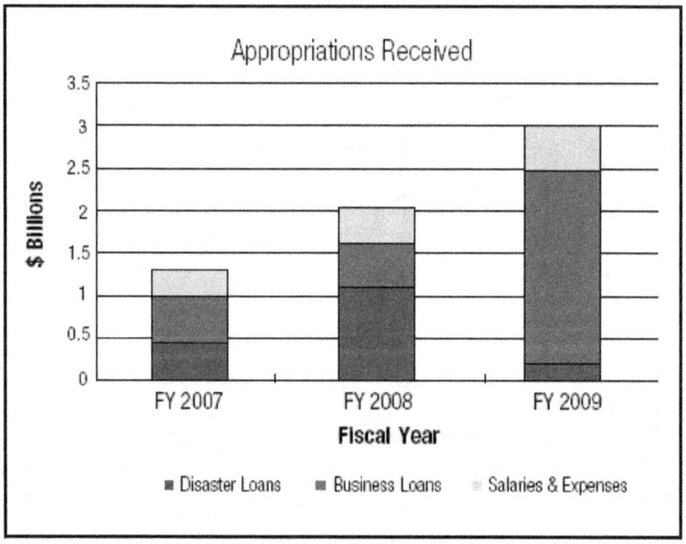

Status of Budgetary Resources

Total Status of Budgetary Resources increased $3.2 billion from FY 2008 to FY 2009. This increase correlates with the increase in the borrowing authority for business loans to cover the increase in purchases as well as the increase in credit program receivables for defaulted guarantied business loans. The SBA expects to continue to see an increase in obligations related to purchases of defaulted guarantied business loans due to the downturn in the economy.

ANALYSIS OF SYSTEMS, CONTROLS AND LEGAL COMPLIANCE

The fourth MD&A section listed in SFFAS 15, ***systems, controls, and legal compliance***, should briefly discuss the status of systems, controls, and legal compliance and describe material problems revealed by audits or otherwise known to management and the corrective actions taken. The volume of information in this section can become excessive. Being concise here is difficult but essential for communicating effectively.

This section should also address any non-compliance with laws and regulations significant to the financial statements (prompt pay, debt collection, anti-deficiency, FFMIA, etc.).

General Services Administration

For FY 2009, the General Services Administration's (GSA) financial report was fully Web-based and presented a very "user friendly" and concise analysis of systems, controls and legal compliance. See the menu selection for "Assurances and Management Challenges" at the Web address listed in Table 1 above, the first page of which is as follows.

Statement of Assurance

The management of the U.S. General Services Administration (GSA) recognizes and fully embraces our responsibility to establish and maintain effective internal controls and financial management systems that meet the objectives of the Federal Managers' Financial Integrity Act (FMFIA). Management assures the effectiveness of GSA's internal controls to support effective and efficient programmatic operations, reliable reporting, and compliance with all applicable laws and regulations. Throughout the year, management conducts extensive evaluation and review of its operations. Based on the results of this effort, GSA can provide reasonable assurance that the objectives of FMFIA are being met, and that no material weaknesses exist in the design or operation of the internal controls as of September 30, 2009.

In addition, GSA conducted an assessment of the effectiveness of internal controls over financial reporting in accordance with Appendix A, Office of Management and Budget's (OMB) Circular A-123, *Management's Responsibility for Internal Control*. Based on the results of this assessment, GSA can provide reasonable assurance that its internal controls over financial reporting, as of June 30, 2009, were operating effectively and no material weaknesses were found in the design or operation of the internal control over financial reporting. The assessment did find that a Federal Financial Management Improvement Act (FFMIA) non-compliance had existed in accounting adjustments being entered at a summary level, resulting in a FFMIA non-compliance with recording the U.S. Standard General Ledger (USSGL) at the transaction level. Subsequent testing through September 30, 2009 identified the remediation of the FFMIA non-compliance due to a successful Lean Six Sigma project implementation. GSA's financial management systems were in substantial compliance with the requirements of FFMIA as of September 30, 2009.

This system of internal controls is also being used to support the American Recovery and Reinvestment Act (Recovery Act) of 2009 awards made at GSA. Relying on OMB guidance, GSA performed an assessment of risks related to the Recovery Act. This assessment, combined with management's assessment of internal controls, enables GSA to provide reasonable assurance that the key accountability objectives of the Recovery Act are being met and that significant risks to meeting these Recovery Act accountability objectives are adequately mitigated.

Paul F. Prouty
Acting Administrator
November 12, 2009

Patent and Trademark Office

The Patent and Trademark Office (PTO) presented a very effective, Web-based analysis of systems controls and legal compliance as follows.

Management Assurances and Compliance with Laws and Regulations

This section provides information on the USPTO's compliance with the following legislative mandates:

- Federal Managers' Financial Integrity Act (FMFIA)
- Federal Financial Management Improvement Act (FFMIA)
- Federal Information Security Management Act
- Inspector General (IG) Act Amendments
- OMB Financial Management Indicators
- Prompt Payment Act
- Civil Monetary Penalty Act
- Debt Collection Improvement Act
- Biennial Review of Fees

Management Assurances

FEDERAL MANAGERS' FINANCIAL INTEGRITY ACT

The FMFIA requires Federal agencies to provide an annual statement of assurance regarding management controls and financial systems. The USPTO management is responsible for establishing and maintaining effective internal control and financial management systems that meet the objectives of the FMFIA. The objectives of internal control, as defined by the Government Accountability Office (GAO), are to ensure:

- Effectiveness and efficiency of operations;
- Reliability of financial reporting; and
- Compliance with laws and regulations.

The statement of assurance is provided at right. This statement was based on the review and consideration of a wide variety of evaluations, control assessments, internal analyses, reconciliations, reports, and other information, including the DOC OIG audits, and the independent public accountants' opinion on the USPTO's financial statements and their reports on internal control and compliance with laws and regulations. In addition, USPTO is not identified on the GAO's High Risk List related to controls governing various areas.

FEDERAL FINANCIAL MANAGEMENT IMPROVEMENT ACT

The FFMIA requires Federal agencies to report on agency substantial compliance with Federal financial management system requirements, Federal accounting standards, and the U.S. Standard General Ledger at the transaction level. The USPTO complied substantially with the FFMIA for FY 2009.

Other Compliance with Laws and Regulations

FEDERAL INFORMATION SECURITY MANAGEMENT ACT

The USPTO continues to stay vigilant in reviewing administrative controls over information systems and is always seeking methods of improving our security program. During FY 2009, the USPTO removed the IT security material weakness that was reported in previous years. The material weakness was related to the USPTO IT security program and reflected the need to improve the internal controls and program processes and procedures for C&A of the USPTO and contractor systems. During FY 2009, the OIG indicated that the USPTO's process for certifying contractor and government systems produced sufficient information to enable the authorizing officials to make credible risk-based accreditation decisions.

On the basis of the USPTO's comprehensive internal control program during FY 2009, the USPTO can provide reasonable assurance that its internal control over the effectiveness and efficiency of operations and compliance with applicable laws and regulations as of September 30, 2009, was operating effectively. Accordingly, I am pleased to certify with reasonable assurance that our agency's systems of internal control, taken as a whole, comply with Section 2 of the Federal Managers' Financial Integrity Act of 1982. Our agency also is in substantial compliance with applicable federal accounting standards and the U.S. Standard General Ledger at the transaction level and with federal financial system requirements. Accordingly, our agency fully complies with Section 4 of the Federal Managers' Financial Integrity Act of 1982, with no material non-conformances.

In addition, the USPTO conducted its assessment of the effectiveness of our agency's internal control over financial reporting, which includes safeguarding of assets and compliance with applicable laws and regulations, in accordance with OMB Circular A-123, Management's Responsibility for Internal Control. Based on the results of this evaluation, the USPTO provides reasonable assurance that its internal control over financial reporting as of June 30, 2009 was operating effectively and no material weaknesses were found in the design or operation of the internal control over financial reporting. In addition, no material weaknesses related to internal control over financial reporting were identified between July 1, 2009 and September 30, 2009.

David J. Kappos

David J. Kappos
Under Secretary of Commerce for Intellectual Property and Director of the United States Patent and Trademark Office
November 5, 2009

INSPECTOR GENERAL ACT AMENDMENTS

The Inspector General Act, as amended, requires semi-annual reporting on IG audits and related activities, as well as any requisite agency follow-up. The report is required to provide information on the overall progress on audit follow-up and internal management controls, statistics on audit reports with disallowed costs, and statistics on audit reports with funds put to better use. The USPTO did not have audit reports with disallowed costs or funds put to better use.

The USPTO's follow-up actions on audit findings and recommendations are essential to improving the effectiveness and efficiency of our programs and operations. As of September 30, 2009, management had resolved the two recommendations outstanding from a report issued in FY 2008 (USPTO-CAR-18701: "USPTO Has Reasonable Controls Over Personal Property, but Additional Improvements Are Needed"). A summary of audit findings and recommendations follows.

Two new audit reports were issued during FY 2009 (ATL-9999-9-3418: "International Intellectual Property Institute (IIPI), DC, Audit of MOU No. 2006-069-039" and ATL-9999-8-3178/ATL-9999-8-3179: "IIPI, DC, Audit of MOU 2004-141-007"). For details on each audit, refer to page 35. No recommendations were outstanding as of September 30, 2009.

Status of IG Act Amendment Audit Recommendations as of September 30, 2009

Report for Fiscal Year	Status	Recommendation	Action Plan	Completion Date
FY 2008	Closed	Conduct inventories consistent with the requirements contained in the Department Personal Property Management Manual dated October 2007.	The USPTO implemented and communicated USPTO's Standard Operating Procedures (SOP) for the annual physical verification of USPTO's home use assets, including laptops.	October 2008
FY 2008	Closed	Require Property Accountability Officers (PAOs) to inventory the holdings of the Property Custodians (PC) who report them.	PAOs received a notice indicating that, as part of their quarterly certification efforts, they must also verify the accuracy of the property assigned to PCs under their oversight.	October 2008

Financial Performance Measure	FY 2009 Target	FY 2009 Performance
Percentage of Timely Vendor Payments (MTS)	98%	96%
Percentage of Payroll by Electronic Transfer (OMB)	90%	99%
Percentage of Treasury Agency Locations Fully Reconciled (OMB)	95%	100%
Timely Reports to Central Agencies (OMB)	95%	100%
Audit Opinion on FY 2009 Financial Statements (OMB)	Unqualified	Unqualified
Material Weaknesses Reported by OIG (OMB)	None	None
Timely Posting of Inter-Agency Charges (USPTO)	30 days	15 days
Average Processing Time for Travel Payments (USPTO)	8 days	4 days

OMB FINANCIAL MANAGEMENT INDICATORS

The OMB prescribes the use of quantitative indicators to monitor improvements in financial management. The USPTO tracks other financial performance measures as well. The table above shows the USPTO's performance during FY 2009 against performance targets established internally and by OMB and the government-wide Metric Tracking System (MTS).

PROMPT PAYMENT ACT

The Prompt Payment Act requires Federal agencies to report on their efforts to make timely payments to vendors, including interest penalties for late payments. In FY 2009, the USPTO did not pay interest penalties on 99.5 percent of the 7,532 vendor invoices processed, representing payments of approximately $534.0 million. Of the 42 invoices that were not processed in a timely manner, the USPTO was required to pay interest penalties on 39 invoices, and was not required to pay interest penalties on three invoices, where the interest was calculated at less than $1. The USPTO paid only $8 in interest penalties for every million dollars disbursed in FY 2009. Virtually all recurring payments were processed by EFT in accordance with the EFT provisions of the Debt Collection Improvement Act of 1996.

CIVIL MONETARY PENALTY ACT

There were no Civil Monetary Penalties assessed by the USPTO during FY 2009.

DEBT COLLECTION IMPROVEMENT ACT

The Debt Collection Improvement Act prescribes standards for the administrative collection, compromise, suspension, and termination of Federal agency collection actions, and referral to the proper agency for litigation. Although the Act has no material effect on the USPTO since it operates with minimal delinquent debt, all debt more than 180 days old has been transferred to the U.S. Department of the Treasury for cross-servicing.

BIENNIAL REVIEW OF FEES

The Chief Financial Officers Act of 1990 requires a biennial review of agency fees, rents, and other charges imposed for services and things of value it provides to specific beneficiaries as opposed to the American public in general. The objective of the review is to identify such activities and to begin charging fees, where permitted by law, and to periodically adjust existing fees to reflect current costs or market value so as to minimize general taxpayer subsidy of specialized services or things of value (such as rights or privileges) provided directly to identifiable non-Federal beneficiaries. The USPTO is a fully fee-funded agency without subsidy of general taxpayer revenue. For non-legislative fees, it uses Activity Based Cost (ABC) accounting to evaluate the costs of activities and determine if fees are set appropriately. When necessary, fees are adjusted to be consistent with the program and with the legislative requirement to recover full cost of the goods or services provided to the public.

In October 2008, the USPTO implemented an increase to patent processing fees, commensurate with the last 12 months' increase in the Consumer Price Index. A study and analysis of all USPTO fees is underway, comparing the average unit costs for all products and services to the fees currently charged. This study is ongoing and is expected to continue through FY 2010.

United States Department of Agriculture

In FY 2009, the Agriculture Department (USDA) presented a summary of the material weaknesses it is working to correct in a concise table as follows.

Federal Managers' Financial Integrity Act Report on Management Control

BACKGROUND

The Federal Managers' Financial Integrity Act (FMFIA) requires ongoing evaluations of internal control and financial management systems. These evaluations lead to an annual statement of assurance that:

- Obligations and costs comply with applicable laws and regulations;
- Federal assets are safeguarded against fraud, waste, and mismanagement;
- Transactions are accounted for and properly recorded; and
- Financial management systems conform to standards, principles, and other requirements to ensure that Federal managers have timely, relevant, and consistent financial information for decision-making purposes.

USDA annually evaluates its internal controls over financial reporting in accordance with OMB Circular A-123, "Management's Responsibility for Internal Control," Appendix A, "Internal Control Over Financial Reporting" (A-123, Appendix A).

The Department operates a comprehensive internal control program. This program ensures compliance with the requirements of FMFIA and other laws and OMB Circulars A–123, Appendix A, and A–127, "Financial Management Systems." All USDA managers must ensure that their programs operate efficiently and effectively, and comply with relevant laws. They must also ensure that financial management systems conform to applicable laws, standards, principles, and related requirements. In conjunction with OIG and GAO, the Department's management works aggressively to determine the root causes of its material weaknesses so that it can direct resources to focus on their remediation.

USDA remains committed to reducing and eliminating the risks associated with its deficiencies. It also strives to efficiently and effectively operate its programs in compliance with FMFIA.

FY 2009 Results

USDA has three existing material weaknesses: Information Technology, Financial Reporting – Unliquidated Obligations, and Financial Reporting – Credit Reform. There is one system non-conformance: Funds Control Management. Thus, the "Secretary's Statement of Assurance" provides qualified assurance that USDA's system of internal control complies with FMFIA objectives. The following exhibit summarizes the results reported in USDA's Consolidated Financial Statements Audit Report.

An auditor-identified deficiency for Rural Development (RD) was found relating to the assumption curves used in cash flow models to perform the annual reestimate calculations. While various processes are in place to ensure the accuracy and completeness of the assumption curves, the overall controls surrounding these processes need improvements to prevent errors.

Exhibit 4: Summary of Financial Statement Audit

Audit Opinion	Unqualified					
Restatement	No					
Material Weakness	Beginning Balance	New	Resolved	Consolidated	Reassessed	Ending Balance
Improvement Needed in Overall Financial Management	1					1
Improvements Needed in Information Technology Security and Controls	1					1
TOTAL MATERIAL WEAKNESSES	2					2

The following exhibit lists USDA's material weaknesses and the financial system non-conformance as related to management's assurance for FMFIA and the certification for FFMIA.

Exhibit 5: Summary of Management Assurances

Effectiveness of Internal Control Over Financial Reporting (FMFIA § 2)						
Statement of Assurance	Qualified					
Material Weakness	Beginning Balance	New	Resolved	Consolidated	Reassessed	Ending Balance
Information Technology	1					1
Financial Reporting - Unliquidated Obligations	1					1
Financial Reporting – Credit Reform	1					1
TOTAL MATERIAL WEAKNESSES	3					3
Effectiveness of Internal Control Over Operations (FMFIA § 2)						
Statement of Assurance	Unqualified					
Material Weakness	Beginning Balance	New	Resolved	Consolidated	Reassessed	Ending Balance
TOTAL MATERIAL WEAKNESSES	0					0
Conformance with Financial Management System Requirements (FMFIA § 4)						
Statement of Assurance	Qualified					
Material Weakness	Beginning Balance	New	Resolved	Consolidated	Reassessed	Ending Balance
Funds Control Management	1					1
TOTAL NON-CONFORMANCE	1					1

Compliance with Federal Financial Management Improvement Act (FFMIA)				
	Agency		Auditor	
Overall Substantial Compliance	No		No	
1. System Requirements	No		No	
2. Accounting Standards	No		No	
3. United States Standard General Ledger at Transaction Level	No		No	
4. Information security policies, procedures, and practices	No		No	

MATERIAL WEAKNESSES

Summary of Outstanding Material Weaknesses

Material Weakness Existing	1. USDA Information Technology	Overall Estimated Completion Date	FY 2012
	Internal control design and operating effectiveness deficiencies in four areas: logical access controls, configuration management, physical access and environmental protection, and disaster recovery. These deficiencies represent an overall Information Technology (IT) material weakness.		
FY 2009 Accomplishments:		**FY 2010 Planned Actions:**	
• Began implementing whole disk encryption on portable computers; • Implemented a Department-wide end-point management software tool ensure complete and timely weakness remediation, improve client management, and ensure compliance with security standards; • Established secure coding requirements and improved application coding by providing a Department-wide tool to ensure compliance; • Improved access controls through dual-factor authentication for network and remote access; • Improved network and boundary protections through a Department Security Operations Center; • Updated regulations to meet the National Institute of Standards and Technology and other Federal requirements relating to change control processes; • Established an Identity and Access Management team to implement a Department-wide approach toward improving and automating access and segregation of duties controls; and • Conducted a policy gap analysis and revised access control and configuration management policies and procedures.		• Expand encryption to include mobile media such as USB thumb drives by the end of the fiscal year; • Finalize deployment of the Department-wide end-point management tool; • Expand the Department-wide Security Operations Center incorporating 24/7 border protection and monitoring, end point compliance, and improved incident response processes; • Establish improved and sustainable processes and procedures for identity and access management; • Standardize the configuration management and change control processes through improved processes and procedures; • Improve the A-123 and FISMA monitoring and reporting process to ensure weaknesses are timely identified and corrected; and • Establish functional disaster recovery site for mainframe and critical mid-range systems.	

Material Weakness Existing	2. Financial Reporting – Unliquidated Obligations	Overall Estimated Completion Date	FY 2010
	Lack of consistent review and follow-up on unliquidated obligations (ULO).		
FY 2009 Accomplishments:		**FY 2010 Planned Actions:**	
• Revised Departmental guidance to require quarterly reviews and certifications for obligations; • Established ULO data mart and aging report for management review and monitoring; • Established ULO Department-wide working group to monitor open obligations, share best practices, and measure agency performance; • Completed statistical sampling of aged ULOs to identify root causes of invalid ones and formulate corrective actions; and • Monitored agency compliance with revised Departmental guidance on quarterly reviews and certifications for obligations.		• Modify systems and related policies, procedures and processes to improve the management, review, and closeout of ULOs; • Conduct training on new processes to manage, review, and closeout ULOs; • Implement automated controls to deobligate invalid ULOs; and • Institute continuous monitoring of controls over ULOs at successive levels of management.	

Material Weakness Existing	3. Financial Reporting – Credit Reform	Overall Estimated Completion Date	FY 2010
	Controls are lacking in the credit reform quality assurance process to ensure that cash flow models, data inputs, estimates, and reestimates are subject to appropriate management oversight.		
FY 2009 Accomplishments:		**FY 2010 Planned Actions:**	
CCC: • Established a team to review all model changes to include members of both the budget and the accounting disciplines. Invited OIG to all Configuration Control Board meetings to monitor CCC's efforts; • Established a timeline for all model changes to allow adequate time for testing and review prior to delivery to the auditors; • Tested all model changes/development results to ensure that model outputs properly capture all elements of the cash flow, not just those affected by change(s) in OMB's Credit Subsidy Calculator 2 to ensure that those results do not produce unintended consequences; and • Procured a contractor for Independent Verification and Validation review and oversight for any newly developed models. USDA: • Reinstituted the Credit Reform Working Group to improve communication and address issues related to credit reform budgeting and accounting; and • Coordinated consistent application of new credit reform guidance. *Note: CCC reported an auditor-identified weakness in controls for the credit reform assurance process in FY 2008. Better procedures were needed to ensure that cash flow models, data inputs, estimates, and reestimates were performed with appropriate management oversight. The material weakness for financial reporting - credit reform has been resolved for CCC.		RD will: • Ensure that detailed second party review procedures are performed and documented by personnel independent of those preparing the assumption curves; • Establish process improvements for version control related to the curves; • Evaluate automation support to determine the feasibility of performing curve calculations systematically; • Enhance review procedures over the quality and accuracy of Cohort Sheet materials; and • Determine the reasonableness of the curves for reestimation purposes and also focus on accuracy of the calculations and portfolio trends.	

Summary of Outstanding System Non-Conformance

System Non-Conformance Existing	1. Funds Control Management	Overall Estimated Completion Date	FY 2012
	System improvements needed in recording obligations at the transactions level.		
FY 2009 Accomplishments:		**FY 2010 Planned Actions:**	
• Developed functionality in the electronic Funds Management System (eFMS) to process funds control at the time of obligation request from FSA/CCC program applications; and • Began acquisition and planning phase of Farm Program Payment System/Modernize and Innovate the Delivery of Agriculture Systems (MIDAS).		• Enhance the eFMS by incorporating transaction level obligations for the Tobacco Transition Payment Program, Direct Payments, and Conservation Reserve Program (CRP) Annual Rental programs that will check funds availability at the time of obligation; • Implement Web-based Supply Chain Management (WBSCM) to integrate obligation transactions for the Commodity Credit Corporation (CCC) Commodity Operations programs into eFMS; and • Complete planning phase and begin software and acquisition phase of MIDAS project.	

Federal Financial Management Improvement Act Report on Financial Management Systems

Background

The Federal Financial Management Improvement Act (FFMIA) is designed to improve financial and program managers' accountability, provide better information for decision-making, and improve the efficiency and effectiveness of Federal programs. FFMIA requires that financial management systems provide reliable, consistent disclosure of financial data in accordance with generally accepted accounting principles and standards. These systems must also comply substantially with: 1) Federal Financial Management System requirements; 2) applicable Federal accounting standards; and 3) the United States Standard General Ledger (USSGL) at the transaction level. Additionally, FISMA requires that there be no significant weaknesses in information security policies, procedures or practices to be substantially compliant with FFMIA (referred to as Section 4 in the accompanying table).

Exhibit 6: Initiatives To Be Completed

Outstanding Initiatives to Achieve FFMIA Compliance			
Initiative	Section of Non-compliance	Agency	Target Completion Date
Information Technology[1]	Federal financial system requirements, and Information security policies, procedures, and/or practices.	Multiple	9/30/2012
Funds Control Management	Federal Financial System requirements.	CCC	10/31/2012
	U.S. Standard General Ledger at the transaction level, and Federal financial management system requirements.	FS	10/1/2010
	Federal financial management system requirements, Federal Accounting Standards, and U.S. Standard General Ledger at the transaction level.	NRCS	12/31/2009

[1] The information technology material weakness, which is reported in the Federal Managers' Financial Integrity Act Report on Management Control, is comprised of four issues: logical access controls, configuration management, physical access and environmental protection, and disaster recovery.

FY 2009 Results

During FY 2009, USDA evaluated its financial management systems to assess substantial compliance with the Act. In assessing FFMIA compliance, the Department considered auditors opinions on component agencies' financial statements, and progress made in addressing the material weaknesses identified in the FY 2008 Performance and Accountability Report. The Department is not compliant with Federal Financial Management System requirements, Federal accounting standards, and the standard general ledger at the transaction level. Additionally, as reported in the FMFIA section of this report, USDA continues to have weaknesses in information technology controls that result in non-compliance with the FISMA requirement. As part of USDA's financial systems strategy, USDA agencies continue working to meet FFMIA and FISMA objectives.

FS is working to mitigate auditor-identified deficiencies related to its systems and methodologies to comply with USSGL at the transaction level and Federal financial management system requirements.

NRCS is working to mitigate auditor-identified deficiencies. Financial management systems did not substantially comply with Federal financial management system requirements, the USSGL at the transaction level, and applicable Federal Accounting Standards for internal use software (including work in progress), undelivered orders, unfilled customer orders, expense accruals, and capital leases. Deficiencies were also noted regarding proper use of USSGL.

Federal Financial Management System Requirements

CCC continues to develop an integrated funds control system, the electronic Funds Management System (eFMS), within the FSA/CCC Core financial management system. This work includes integration with CCC's general ledger system at the transaction level. eFMS will also provide management with timely information to monitor and control the status of budgetary resources recorded in the general ledger.

FY 2009 accomplishments included:

- Developed functionality in eFMS to process funds control at the time of obligation request from FSA/CCC program applications; and
- Began Acquisition and Planning phase of Farm Program Payment System/Modernize and Innovate the Delivery of Agriculture Systems (MIDAS).

In FY 2010, CCC will:

- Enhance eFMS by incorporating transaction level obligations for the Tobacco Transition Payment Program, Direct Payments, and CRP Annual Rental programs that will check funds availability at the time of obligation;
- Implement Web-based Supply Chain Management (WBSCM) to integrate obligation transactions for CCC Commodity Operations programs into eFMS; and
- Complete Planning phase and begin Software and Acquisition phase of MIDAS.

In FY 2011 CCC will:

- Complete Proof of Concept and System Design for MIDAS.

In FY 2012, CCC will:

- Complete software modifications to program applications to send obligation transactions for CCC Farm, Foreign, and remaining commodity operations programs;
- Implement Financial Management Modernization Initiative and FSA's Modernize and Innovate the Delivery of Agricultural Systems packages; and
- Begin Initial Operating Capability for MIDAS.

FORWARD-LOOKING INFORMATION, TRENDS, AND MANAGEMENT CHALLENGES

"***Forward-looking information***" in the MD&A is arguably the most useful information management can provide. The MD&A should discuss the expected future effects of current demands, risks, uncertainties, events, conditions, and trends, and it should discuss the expected future effects of anticipated events, conditions, and trends, which SFFAS 15 encourages but does not require. Forward-looking information may be in any of the four MD&A sections.

Federal Housing Finance Agency

In the performance section of the Federal Housing Finance Agency's (FHFA) FY 2009 MD&A, the FHFA use forward-looking information as follows.

> #### Mortgage Delinquencies and Defaults
>
> Rapidly rising levels of serious delinquencies and defaults, further aggravated by high levels of unemployment and severe declines in home prices, continue to stress the Enterprises. As of June 30, 2009, Enterprise serious delinquencies had increased nearly 200 percent year-over-year to 2.89 percent for Freddie Mac and 3.94 percent for Fannie Mae. Real estate owned (REO) acquisitions for the first three quarters of FY 2009 at Fannie Mae were 57,469, an approximate 30 percent increase year-over-year. Freddie Mac had 35,987 REO acquisitions, approximately 60 percent higher than the year before.
>
> To mitigate the impact of continued serious delinquencies and defaults, the Enterprises expanded loan modification efforts and took leadership roles in the MHA program. The FHL Banks that participate in mortgage purchase programs developed borrower assistance programs that enhance the foreclosure prevention efforts for mortgage loans owned by the FHL Banks.
>
> The Enterprises are recording historic levels of modifications and refinances. For borrowers unable to continue homeownership, the Enterprises offer foreclosure alternatives, including short sales, deeds in lieu of foreclosure, and REO rental programs. The impact of the HAMP and HARP elements remains uncertain as unemployment and house prices continue to deteriorate, interest rates rise from historic lows, other initiatives are set to expire, and operational difficulties in implementing foreclosure prevention programs arise.
>
> #### Operational Challenges Facing the Enterprises
>
> FHFA placed both Enterprises into conservatorship in September 2008 because deteriorating market conditions threatened the companies' ability to fulfill their mission. The Enterprises continue to be challenged by operational constraints both internally and by counterparties. To handle high numbers of loan modifications, loan servicers are making significant changes in their operational

systems. In addition, servicers are increasing personnel to meet the intensive labor demands needed to manage and reduce foreclosures. The Enterprises are working with the government and servicers to accelerate loan modifications and refinancing, but they also must improve systems within their own operations and coordinate changes with servicers.

In 2008 Treasury established three finance facilities (GSE Credit Facility, MBS Purchase Program, and Senior Preferred Stock Purchase Agreement) to support the ongoing business operations of the Enterprises and meet conservatorship objectives. These facilities support the Enterprises' capital and liquidity to provide confidence to investors in the Enterprises' debt and MBS. Some of these facilities expire at the end of this year, so the Enterprises and FHFA are working with Treasury to ensure investor confidence is maintained through appropriate government support coupled with strengthened liquidity and asset liability management within the Enterprises.

Postal Service

The Postal Service revenue must cover expenditures and therefore the Postal Service must project future activity and set rates. The following is from the "Risk Factors" section of the Postal Service financial report preceding the MD&A but would be suitable for the MD&A.

> *Adverse changes in the economy directly impact our business, negatively affecting our results of operations.*
>
> The demand for postal services is heavily influenced by the economy. We are now in the early stages of a recovery, though most economists believe that it will be slow and prolonged. However the nature of the recovery is not universal. U.S. national unemployment, on the increase since January 2008, reached 9.8% by the close of our fiscal year on September 30, 2009, and 10.2% in October, the highest level since 1983. Unemployment may continue to rise for the next several quarters in spite of the anticipated growth in gross domestic product (GDP). The lingering effects of turmoil in the financial markets have resulted in a crisis of confidence among consumers, which raises economic risk significantly. Uncertain market conditions are expected to have an adverse impact on retail sales, investment, consumer spending and consumer confidence. Negative trends in these areas are likely to depress the demand for postal services.

And from the Postal Service MD&A per se:

CAUTIONARY STATEMENTS

Forward-looking statements contained in this report represent our best estimates of trends we know about, trends we anticipate and trends we believe are relevant to future operations. However, actual results may be different from estimates. Certain forward-looking statements are included in this report and use such words as "may," "will," "could," "expect," "believe," "plan" or other similar terminology. These statements reflect current expectations regarding future events and operating performance as of the date of this report. These forward-looking statements involve a number of risks and uncertainties.

The following are some of the factors that could cause actual results to differ materially from those expressed in, or underlying, forward-looking statements: effectiveness of operating initiatives; success in advertising and promotional efforts; changes in national and local business and economic conditions, including their impact on consumer and business confidence; fluctuations in currency exchange and interest rates; labor and other operating costs; oil, fuel and other transportation costs; the effects of war and terrorist activities; competition, including pricing and marketing initiatives and new service offerings by our competitors; consumer preferences or perceptions concerning our service offerings; spending patterns and demographic trends; availability of qualified personnel; severe weather conditions; effects of legal claims; cost and deployment of capital; changes in laws and regulations; costs and delays associated with new regulations imposed by the PRC; and changes in applicable accounting policies and practices. The foregoing list of important factors is not all-inclusive. We have no obligation to publicly update or revise any forward-looking statements, whether as a result of new information, future events or otherwise.

MD&A Best Practices – Forward-looking Information, Trends, and Management Challenges

From the Postal Service MD&A, page 35:

> We believe that our liquidity and cash flows will cover operation through most of 2010, but we remain highly uncertain regarding the availability of cash in an amount that is sufficient to fund our required $5.5 billion PSRHBF payment on September 30, 2010. If sufficient cash is not available, we will not be able to make the full payment. The legal and/or regulatory consequences of failing to make the required PSRHBF payment cannot be known with certainty. We will continue to inform the Congress on our financial outlook and on legislative changes that would help ensure the availability of cash at September 30, 2010. However, there can be no assurance that adjustments to the PSRHBF payment schedule will be granted by September 30, 2010, or at all.

Patent and Trademark Office

The Patent and Trademark Office's (PTO) presents forward-looking information in the MD&A section entitled "Management Challenges and What's Ahead", as follows.

Management Challenges and What's Ahead

The USPTO will continue to lead the world in IP policy by optimizing patent and trademark quality and timeliness, and improving IP protection and enforcement domestically and abroad by addressing the following challenges:

MAKE EFFICIENCY GAINS FOR THE FUTURE, WHILE KEEPING QUALITY HIGH

The Patent and Trademark organizations will build on their accomplishments and work toward meeting the objectives of the ***2007-2012 Strategic Plan*** while working with customers to ensure that the objectives remain aligned with their needs.

The Patent organization's biggest challenge is to address the growth of pendency and the backlog of patent applications waiting to be examined while maintaining high patent quality. The Patent organization must address the dual challenges of heavy workloads and a shift of applications from traditional arts to more complex technologies. Consequently, the Patent organization will continue to hire, train, and retain additional examiners, and explore and implement process improvements. These actions will help to make the Agency even more responsive to the ever-increasing demand for patents.

The Trademark organization must strike a proper balance between forecasting levels of new filings, existing inventories, and managing an appropriately sized staff to ensure sufficient resources are available to maintain pendency goals on a consistent basis. The Trademark business' biggest challenge is to maintain the gains it has made in quality and pendency given the uncertainty of trademark filings, future revenues, and controlling costs. Efficiency gains have been realized through process improvement and cost reduction along with greater use of information technology. First-action pendency has reached the long-term target range of 2.5 to 3.5 months. Maintaining first-action pendency on a consistent monthly basis, given monthly fluctuations in filings, the unpredictability of projecting new filings given the continued uncertainty of the economy and the need to secure congressional approval for funding to support a high quality operation presents any number of challenges that must be carefully managed.

The Trademark organization will continue to assess the efficiency of its operations going forward, and incorporate process improvement in the incremental redesign of the electronic workflow and file management system. Completing the electronic workflow and file management system throughout the entire process will provide better automated tools and consistency for managing workloads and yield better services to its customers. The USPTO will also continue to use e-government as the primary means of doing business with applicants and registrants, and as a means of processing work within the Trademark organization. Continued high quality actions and consistent low first-action pendency will ensure low disposal pendency which translates to certainty for business owners in making investments in new products and services.

The Trademark organization will continue to assess the efficiency of its operations going forward, and incorporate process improvement in the incremental redesign of the electronic workflow and file management system. Completing the electronic workflow and file management system throughout the entire process will provide better automated tools and consistency for managing workloads and yield better services to its customers. The USPTO will also continue to use e-government as the primary means of doing business with applicants and registrants, and as a means of processing work within the Trademark organization. Continued high quality actions and consistent low first-action pendency will ensure low disposal pendency which translates to certainty for business owners in making investments in new products and services.

ECONOMIC AND FINANCIAL UNCERTAINTY

The financial crisis that began last year in the U.S. has created challenges for the USPTO as the world economy has fallen into a recession. The USPTO derives its budgetary resources from user fees and the recent economic downturn impacted patent and trademark operations and revealed vulnerability in the method for financing the Agency. The downturn in patent allowance, maintenance, and application fees stems directly from the financial constraints that even the nation's most innovative companies face.

Patent and Trademark application filings, which historically increase year after year, declined between FY 2008 and 2009. Filing forecasts were lowered in expectation that the downturn in the economy would impact filings and revenues – specifically as they relate to the gross domestic product (GDP) and financial indicators such as venture capital. Continued uncertainty exists for the next two to three years in planning and managing staffing and budget requests that are supported by fee revenues, especially if current fee rates remain unchanged.

The USPTO sought legislation to enable it to temporarily use Trademark unobligated balances through June 2010 to forestall the need for a furlough, if needed. The USPTO is also exploring the use of new financing tools, such as fee setting authority, borrowing authority, operating reserves, and investment authority that would permit adjustment for volatility in the economy and/or demand for products and services without putting the Office in an operational crisis. Such tools would also permit the USPTO to undertake long-term strategies for improvement in a financially reasonable way.

And also, further on in the section --

ENSURING PROPER FEE RATES

Under current authority, any change to statutory fees requires legislation.[1] This limits the USPTO's ability to adjust its fees in response to changes in market demand for patent and trademark services, in processing costs or in other factors. To assure adequate funding levels for the long term, the USPTO needs authority to set and adjust fees administratively, so that it can properly establish and align fees in a timely, fair and consistent manner to recover the actual costs of USPTO operations and without going through the inherently long delays in the legislative process.

Any fee adjustments could be subject to oversight, review and comment by the USPTO's Public Advisory Committees, its stakeholders and Congress. This would provide assurances that the USPTO has all the necessary oversight, checks, and balances.

MD&A Best Practices – Forward-looking Information, Trends, and Management Challenges

Department of Veterans Affairs

Among the MD&A sections provided by the Department of Veterans' Affairs' (VA) Web-based presentation is one on "most important achievements and current challenges." The sample shown immediately below is for VA's strategic goals 1 and 2. It is an effective, frank discussion by strategic goal. Another section is on "performance shortfall analysis", which is also presented immediately below for goals 1 and 2 only. Both sections provide excellent forward-looking information.

Strategic Goal 1

RESTORATION AND IMPROVED QUALITY OF LIFE FOR DISABLED VETERANS

Most Important Achievements

SUICIDE PREVENTION PROGRAM: Further **expansion** of the Veterans **Suicide Hotline** has allowed for an average of over 350 callers a day to access the Hotline and these numbers continue to grow. The addition of the Internet-based Veterans Chat feature has expanded the reach of the Suicide Prevention program to our newer Veterans who may choose to communicate via the Internet. Over **5,000** rescues have been sent out as a result of this outreach program and more importantly almost 20,000 referrals from callers have been sent to the local suicide prevention coordinators in the first 2 years of operation.

TRACKING TOOL FOR SEVERELY ILL AND INJURED: VA implemented a tracking tool for care management of **severely ill** and injured **OEF/OIF Veterans.** The new application, known as the Care Management Tracking and Reporting Application (CMTRA), is a robust, **Web-based** tracking system that allows care managers to specify a **care management** schedule for each individual Veteran and to identify specialty care managers such as Polytrauma Case Managers, Spinal Cord Injury Case Managers, and others. CMTRA also allows the OEF/OIF Care Management team to designate a Lead Case Manager when multiple case managers at the facility level are involved in the Veteran's care. As of August 2009, VA is caring for more than 2,300 severely ill or injured OEF/OIF Veterans.

COMPLETION OF THE GERIATRICS AND EXTENDED CARE STRATEGIC PLAN: This plan will guide **VA service delivery for frail elderly and disabled Veterans through the year 2020.** The plan is based on 82 recommendations, input of 6 workgroups convened in over 100 conference calls over a 4-month period.

EXPANDING THE DISABILITY EVALUATION SYSTEM PILOT PROGRAM: VA expanded the DES pilot program **from 3 sites** in the National Capitol Region **to 21 sites nationwide**. The pilot program, in cooperation with DoD, involves administering **a single medical examination** and assigning a single disability evaluation for active duty persons entering the Medical Evaluation Board process. The goal of the pilot program is to **reduce the overall time** it takes a servicemember to progress through DES from time of referral to the Medical Evaluation Board to receipt of VA benefits.

SURVIVOR BENEFIT CLAIMS PROCESSING CONSOLIDATED: VA completed its consolidation of all survivor benefit claims processing to the three Pension Management Centers in Milwaukee, St. Paul, and Philadelphia. This will **reduce wait time for beneficiaries** and **increase the accuracy and consistency** of VA's claims decisions.

25 PERCENT INCREASE IN SPECIALLY ADAPTED HOUSING GRANTS AWARDED: 1,270 severely **disabled Veterans and servicemembers** now live in new housing or have adapted an existing dwelling to meet their adaptive **housing needs** enabling them to live more independently. This is a **25 percent increase** from 2008.

Strategic Goal 1

Restoration and Improved Quality of Life for Disabled Veterans

Most Important Achievements, *cont'd*

VETERANS' QUALITY OF LIFE IMPROVED THROUGH MORE OUTREACH: The following initiatives were:

- Improved VA's VetSuccess.gov Web site: Veterans can now browse job listings, post resumes, and apply for positions online. VetSuccess.gov allows Veterans to access more than 500,000 job openings. An estimated 27,000 Veterans and 200 employers are registered on VetSuccess.gov.
- Increased outreach to National Guard and Reserve members by collaborating with DoD on two new initiatives: The Post Deployment Health Reassessment Program (PDHRA) and the Yellow Ribbon Reintegration program (YRRP).
  - PDHRA events are **health screening events** designed to address post deployment-related health concerns and readjustment concerns. Servicemembers and Veterans receive evaluations and referrals for follow-up and care.
  - YRRP activities focus on **reconnecting Servicemembers and their families with service providers** and the resources that are available to help them overcome the challenges of reintegration.

Challenges

SUICIDE PREVENTION PROGRAM: Reaching Veterans of all ages requires a variety of approaches and multi-modal outreach strategies. **Communicating with Veterans via the Internet and social networking sites** presents new security problems as well as the development of new types of intervention strategies.

CLAIMS WORKLOAD TO INCREASE: VA received over one million disability compensation and pension claims in 2009. This represents **a 14 percent increase in workload** from 2008 to 2009.

CLAIMS COMPLEXITY: The complexity of claims received continues to increase as more **Veterans are claiming 8 or more chronic progressive conditions** such as orthopedic, mental health, cardiovascular, etc.

DES REQUIRES EXTENSIVE CHANGE: The DES pilot program requires significant changes to business processes and extensive, complex coordination between VA and DoD. For example, **service treatment records are transferred to VA in hard copy** because the infrastructure to transfer the records electronically has yet to be built.

MORE TRAINING AND CONTINUAL TRAINING NEEDED: Consolidation of survivor claims processing requires **ongoing dedication to training newly hired staff** before improvements in efficiency are fully realized.

CONTINUED INCREASE IN SAH WORKLOAD ANTICIPATED: The number of SAH grants **approved increased 75 percent** from 2007 levels because of changes in Public Laws 109-233 and 110-289. These changes included **increased grant amounts**, multiple use provisions, and yearly adjustments to the grant maximums based on a cost-of-construction index.

Strategic Goal 2

Smooth Transition to Civilian Life

Most Important Achievements

Housing for Homeless Veterans: VA, in partnership with the Department of Housing and Urban Development, **provided 20,000 units of permanent supportive housing to homeless Veterans**. As of the end of August 2009, more than 6,300 Veterans have been placed in permanent housing.

31 VA Liaisons Placed in 17 Military Treatment Facilities: VA now has **31 VA Liaisons** strategically placed at 17 Military Treatment Facilities (MTF) with concentrations of recovering servicemembers returning from Afghanistan and Iraq. The VA Liaisons **facilitate the transfer of servicemembers and Veterans** from the MTF to the VA medical center closest to their home or most appropriate for the specialized services their medical condition requires.

Restored Vision for Homeless Veterans: Through this pilot program **more than 620 homeless Veterans received vision care and eye glasses** through donations from Faith-Based and Community Organizations and foundations.

Post-9/11 GI Bill Implemented: On August 1, 2009, the **Post-9/11 GI Bill became law**. VA's successful implementation was made possible because of the following achievements:

- Published 359 pages of new regulations and modified ten existing information technology systems.
- Hired and trained approximately 760 term Veterans Claims Examiners.
- Began accepting applications on May 1, 2009, well before the fall enrollment.
- Started accepting enrollment certifications and processing awards on July 7, 2009.
- Began making payments for the Post-9/11 GI Bill on August 3, 2009.

Challenges

Greater Workload and Automating GI Bill Work: With the implementation of the Post-9/11 GI Bill, VA faces operational challenges including those listed below:

- Managing the increased workload associated with the implementation of the Post-9/11 GI Bill.
- Achieving timeliness targets with limited automation and less experienced claims processing staff.
- Transitioning from an interim IT solution to a long-term IT solution for processing Post-9/11 GI Bill claims.

Preparing Staff for New Challenges: VA must continue to **prepare our military service coordinators for future challenges**, particularly expansion of the DES pilot, expansion of the Benefit Delivery at Discharge and Quick Start programs, and potential deployed support to service personnel in combat zones.

Performance Shortfall Analysis

Shown below (sorted by strategic goal) are brief explanations of the reasons for significant deviations between actual and planned performance for those measures where there were significant shortfalls. Also provided are resolution strategies that are being implemented to ensure goal achievement in the future. These results are coded "red" in the measures tables beginning on page II-144.

Strategic Goal 1 Restoration and Improved Quality of Life for Disabled Veterans			
Measure		Target	Result
National Accuracy Rate for Compensation Rating Claims		**90%**	**83%** Ⓡ
Causes	• Accuracy declined because newly hired employees are not yet fully proficient in analyzing and processing claims. New staff undergo intensive, curriculum-based training that occurs over several months. Not all new staff has completed the full training curriculum and, although training is critical, even when fully completed, new hires need time to achieve maximum proficiency.		
Resolution Strategies	• Once training is completed, new employees are able to gain proficiency with oversight of completed work by more experienced staff. Accuracy will improve as more of the newly-hired employees become fully trained and gain experience and proficiency through the review process. • In 2009, VA began to consolidate survivor benefit claims to the three Pension Management Centers, while Veterans' compensation claims continue to be processed at the regional offices. • Employees at the regional offices will therefore concentrate solely on Veterans' compensation claims. This specialization is expected to improve claims processing accuracy.		
National Accuracy Rate Compensation & Pension Fiduciary Work (This measure supports SG1 and SG3.)		**88%**	**82%** Ⓡ
Causes	• FY 2009 was the first full year that all fiduciary activities for regional offices in the Western Area were consolidated to the Western Area Pilot Fiduciary Hub in Salt Lake City. • Additionally, VBA hired over 20 new Legal Instruments Examiners during FY 2009. • The combination of a large group of new incoming employees and the reorganization of workflow resulted in only a slight gain in accuracy (up from 81 percent in FY 2008).		

Resolution Strategies	• Consolidation provides increased oversight and coordination of one standard for quality for the entire Western Area. VA will document gains in accuracy and efficiencies to determine best practices to use in the other Areas. • Additionally, VA finalized the transition of all fiduciary activities to paperless processing in FY 2009. This transition, along with the additional experience gained by newly added employees, should result in increased accuracy in FY 2010.

Strategic Goal 2
Smooth Transition to Civilian Life

Measure	Target	Result
Number of new enrollees waiting to be scheduled for their first appointment (electronic wait list)	<200	543 Ⓡ

Causes	• The majority of Veterans on the EWL are related to Primary Care (PC). PC serves as a gateway into VA health care, and the increase may be due to the economic downturn and continued influx of newly discharged Veterans from the current conflicts. VHA is seeing an increase of newly enrolled Veterans. • An increase in new enrollees waiting over 30 days is evident in Primary Care. Most new enrollees are initially seen in Primary Care; therefore, there would naturally be a wait in those clinics, especially when enrollment numbers continue to increase.
Resolution Strategies	• We continue to impress upon our providers and clinic staff the need for continued vigilance in practicing and implementing the Advanced Clinical Access (ACA) initiative. • ACA promotes the smooth flow of patients through the clinic process and seeks to minimize wait times by anticipating patient needs at the time of their appointment and taking steps to: ○ Ensure specific equipment is available. ○ Arrange for tests that should be completed either prior to or at the time of the visit. ○ Align patient, provider, and all necessary health information.

Strategic Goal 2 Smooth Transition to Civilian Life			
	Measure	**Target**	**Result**
Telephone activities - Blocked call rate (Education)		**10**	**38** Ⓡ
Causes	The implementation of the Post-9/11 GI Bill created a 15.6 percent increase in claims received from FY 2008 to 2009. The increase, coupled with limited automation for processing claims under the new program and lower efficiency in the greatly expanded workforce, resulted in longer processing times and a higher inventory of pending claims. This, in turn, prompted an increase of 270 percent in telephone traffic for the period April-September 2009 over the corresponding period in 2008.		
Resolution Strategies	In order to reduce processing time and inventory, an additional 760 FTE have been added at the Regional Processing Offices. The number of personnel assigned to the Education Call Center in the Muskogee Regional Processing Office was increased by more than 25 percent. Physical and financial resource constraints prevented further increase in Call Center staffing.		
Telephone activities - Abandoned call rate (Education)		**5**	**11** Ⓡ
Causes	The implementation of the Post-9/11 GI Bill created a 15.6 percent increase in claims received from FY 2008 to 2009. The increase, coupled with limited automation for processing claims under the new program and lower efficiency in the greatly expanded workforce, resulted in longer processing times and a higher inventory of pending claims. This in turn prompted an increase of 270 percent in telephone traffic for the period April-September 2009 over the corresponding period in 2008.		
Resolution Strategies	In order to reduce processing time and inventory, an additional 760 FTE have been added at the Regional Processing Offices. The number of personnel assigned to the Education Call Center in the Muskogee Regional Processing Office was increased by more than 25 percent. Physical and financial resource constraints prevented further increase in Call Center staffing.		

MD&A Best Practices – Forward-looking Information, Trends, and Management Challenges

<u>Department of Energy</u>

The sample shown immediately below is from Energy's Management Priorities and includes how Energy plans to address an area on one of GAO's high risk list.

Leadership Challenges

The Department carries out multiple complex and highly diverse missions. Although the Department is continually striving to improve the efficiency and effectiveness of its programs and operations, there are some specific areas that merit a higher level of focus and attention. These areas oftentimes require long-term strategies for ensuring stable operations and represent the most daunting Leadership Challenges the Department faces in accomplishing its mission.

The Reports Consolidation Act of 2000 requires that, annually, the Inspector General (IG) prepare a statement summarizing what he considers to be the most serious management and performance challenges facing the Department. These challenges are included in the Other Accompanying Information section of this report. Similarly, in FY 2003 the GAO identified six major management challenges and program risks to be addressed by the Department.

The Department, after considering all critical activities within the agency and those areas identified by the IG and GAO, has identified nine Leadership Challenges that represent the most important strategic management issues facing the Department now and in the coming years.

Contract and Project Administration

Key Challenges: The Department has been directed by Congress to take corrective action to be removed from the GAO High Risk List for inadequate contract and project oversight and management. DOE has been on this GAO list since its inception in 1990. The Department will need the support of GAO, OMB and the Department's senior leadership to enact the requisite cultural and policy changes.

Departmental Initiatives: The Department completed a comprehensive Root Cause Analysis of contract and project management deficiencies in April 2008 and approved a Corrective Action Plan (CAP) in July 2008. The measures of CAP address root cause deficiencies by providing solutions and demonstrable results. To strengthen front-end planning, the Department has implemented Project Definition Rating Index and Technology Readiness Assessment Tools. The Department has also developed a staffing model based on Naval Facilities Command and the U.S. Army Corps of Engineers (Corps) best practices, and adopted a policy requiring that projects costing $50 million or less be fully funded by FY 2013.

Implementation of CAP corrective actions will continue in FY 2010. During this time, the Department will:

- Enact a staffing model (algorithm and guide) identifying the approximate types and number of Federal staff necessary for appropriate project oversight during planning and execution phases.
- Develop and deploy a user-friendly replacement Project Assessment and Rating System (PARS) that provides transparent, consistent, and quality project performance data (including contractor Earned Value Management System data) to all levels of field and Headquarters.
- Implement a corporate contract and project management lessons learned system.
- Issue a revision to the Department's project management directive, DOE Order 413.3A.

Corrective measures will be monitored, measured and reported quarterly to senior Departmental, OMB and GAO leadership. In addition, the Department will report CAP status and progress to the House and Senate Appropriations Committees in the annual budget request.

MD&A Best Practices – Forward-looking Information, Trends, and Management Challenges

Social Security Administration (SSA)

The sample shown immediately below is from SSA and includes how they plan to address improper payments.

STRATEGIC OBJECTIVE 4.1: CURB IMPROPE

Our program integrity workloads are critical to ensuring
workloads depends upon resources. Due to the tight bud
service to the public and stewardship efforts. To maintai
stewardship workloads as we described on pages 63 and
reviews. However, we are beginning to reverse the overr
to devote more funds towards such reviews in FY 2010.
improper payments as well as collect debt.

Conduct Supplemental Security Income Redeter
cash assistance to aged, blind, and disabled individuals w
eligible for these benefits, changes in their living arrange
affect their ongoing eligibility for or the amount of their b
payments only to eligible individuals, we conduct period
redeterminations. Redeterminations are a proven investm
the correct amount based on their circumstances such as t
currently estimate that redeterminations processed above
$7 in program savings for each $1 spent, including saving
2,422,000 SSI redeterminations, an increase of more than
redeterminations is a step in the right direction, our progr
were at the beginning of this decade. We attribute our de
number of redeterminations we have been able to comple

Perform Continuing Disability Reviews: To ensu
meet our medical requirements, we periodically conduct
continuing disability reviews are highly productive; every
even more efficient, we continue to refine the continuing
cases and identify those for which a full medical review v
continuing disability reviews for the remaining cases. W
reviews process, which increases our speed and potential
review process.

Initiate Automated International Death Data Ex
automated exchange of death data with a foreign country
and the U.S. provide information to each other electronic
Social Security benefits from the other country. As a res
improper payments can be avoided. We will continue to
expansion.

Expand the *Access to Financial Institutions* Proj
criteria to qualify for SSI benefits. To determine whethe
resources, including those held in financial institutions.
electronically verify account balances and identify undisc
SSI payments.

Our studies indicate that up to four percent of individuals
would result in a denial of benefits. We can obtain bank
exchange compared to current manual processes. We hav
in California, New Jersey, and New York. We plan to ex
ultimate goal of nationwide implementation.

Enhance Overpayment Collection Efforts: We make every effort to recover Social Security and SSI overpayments from the overpaid individual or a representative payee who may be liable for the overpayment. We have several avenues to collect debt. Withholding current benefit payments from the individual is preferable since debt is more difficult to recoup once benefits end; therefore, we make every effort to identify and collect debt as soon as possible. If the overpaid individual no longer receives benefits, we offer the opportunity to repay debt via monthly installment payments. If a repayment agreement cannot be arranged, we withhold debt from a variety of sources including federal tax refunds, federal annuities, and wages. We have enhanced our debt collection process through recovery via offset of state payments, including state tax refunds. In addition, we are exploring other debt-collection tools, such as use of private collection agencies and the application of administrative fees and interest charging.

<u>Department of the Treasury</u>

The sample shown immediately below is from Treasury and includes a summary of both Treasury's performance and financial trend data.

Fiscal Year 2009 Summary of Performance by Strategic Goal

STRATEGIC GOAL	KEY ACCOMPLISHMENTS	KEY CHALLENGES	TREND
U.S. and World Economies Perform at Full Economic Potential Cost: 2008: $3.7 Billion 2009: $4.4 Billion	• Supported stabilization of the financial system through implementation of the *Emergency Economic Stabilization Act of 2008* and the Financial Stability Plan • Improved mortgage availability and stability of the housing market through implementation of the *Housing and Economic Recovery Act of 2008* • Implemented economic stimulus measures under the *American Recovery and Reinvestment Act of 2009* • Issued "Financial Regulatory Reform: A New Foundation" and drafted legislation for fundamental financial regulatory reform • Contributed to stabilization of the money market through implementation of a Temporary Guarantee Program for Money Market Funds • Implemented measures to bolster regulation of national banks and thrifts • Expanded international economic partnerships to better manage the financial crisis • Hosted G-20 meetings and supported elevation of the G-20 to premier international economic forum • Supported trebling resources for the International Monetary Fund and restructuring of the Financial Stability Forum into the Financial Stability Board • Coordinated the Economic Track of the U.S.-China Strategic and Economic Dialogue • Provided grants, investments, financial services and technical support for underserved and low-income communities through the CDFI Fund	• Repair and reform the regulatory system to improve supervision of financial markets and institutions • Continue to mitigate risks at national banks and thrifts • Reduce mortgage delinquency and foreclosure rates • Reduce direct government support for securitization and other financial markets • Maintain open economies despite rising protectionist interests • Reform Medicare and Social Security to ensure long-term solvency • Continue international movement towards a global agreement on climate change • Increase financial knowledge and access, especially in low-income and underserved communities • Improve productivity management related to coin and currency production • Improve supply management for bullion coin production • Manage cost issues related to the penny and nickel • Encourage robust circulation of the $1 coin cost-effectively • Increase financial literacy and access to financial services in low-income and underserved communities	Performance ▼ Budget ▲ Cost ▲

How Well is Treasury Performing?

Treasury Performance Cost Trend

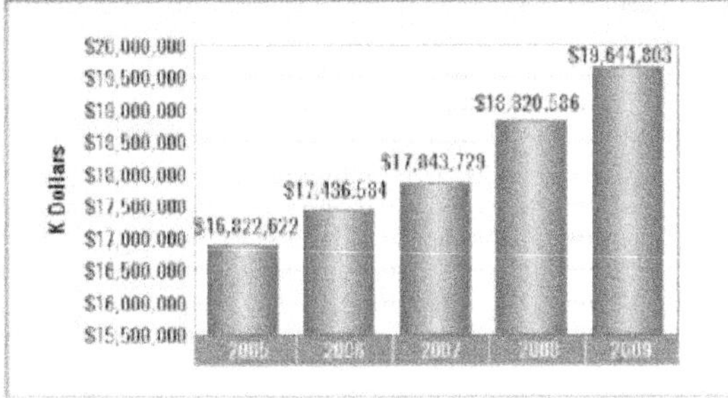

Treasury Total (Direct and Non-Appropriated) Budget Trend

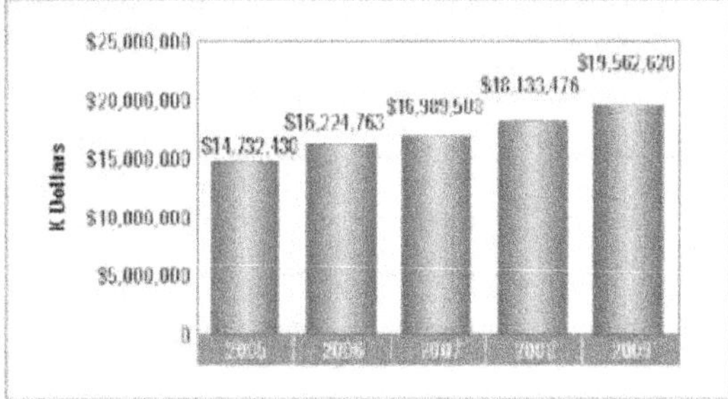

Fiscal Year 2009 Treasury-wide Performance Results Including Discontinued and Baseline Measures

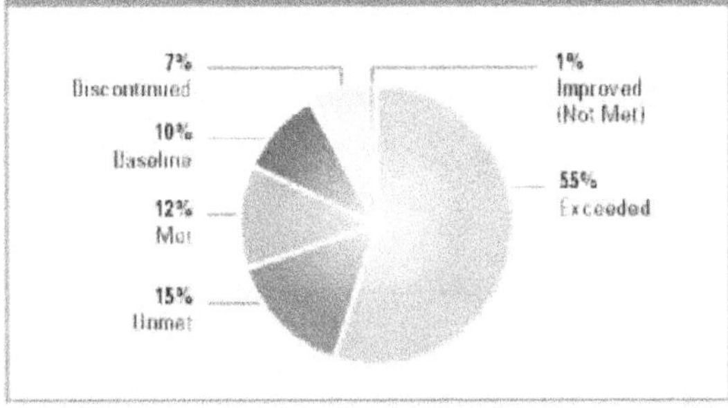

Fiscal Year 2009 Treasury-wide Performance Results Excluding Discontinued and Baseline Measures

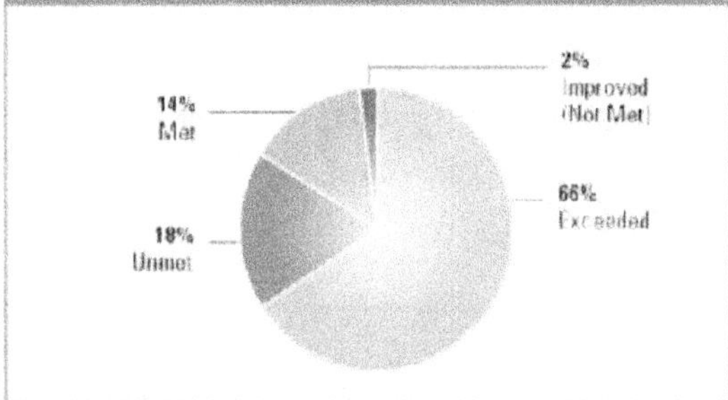

Treasury Actual Performance Trends 2006–2009

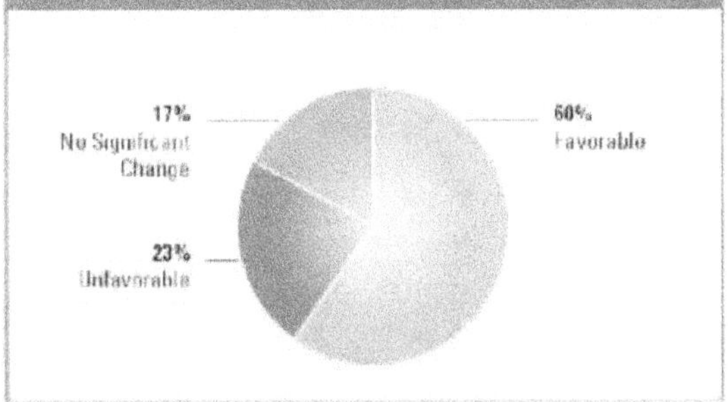

Treasury Target Performance Trends 2006–2009

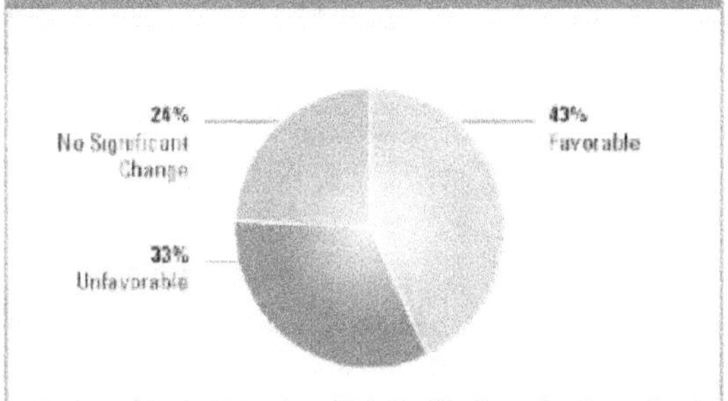

Treasury Department Cost per Person in the United States

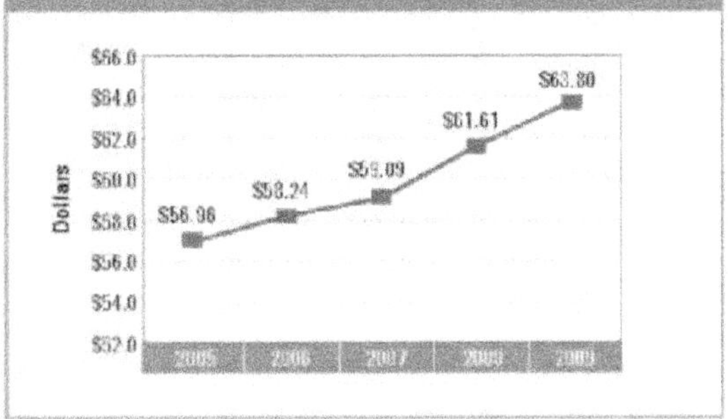

Treasury Performance vs. Performance Cost Trends

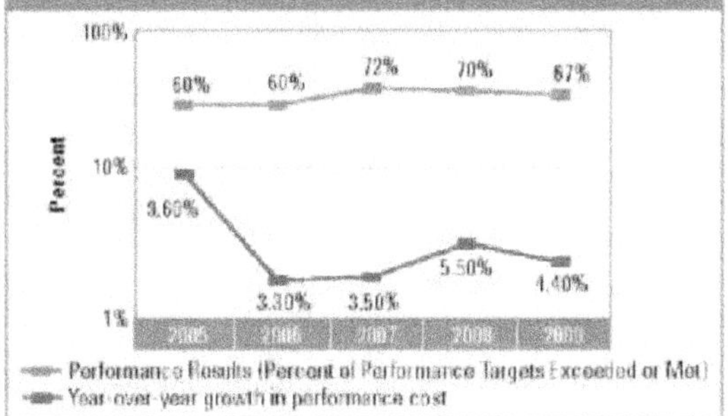

Please see next page for explanation of charts.

Financial Highlights

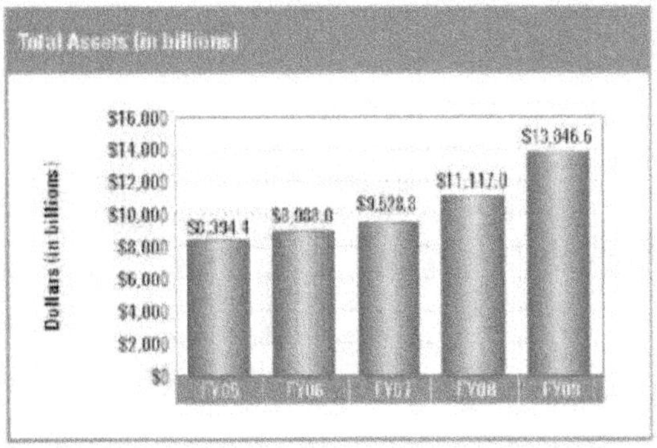

The increase of $2.7 trillion in total assets in fiscal year 2009 is largely due to the increase in future funds required from the General Fund of the U.S. Government to pay for the federal debt owed to the public and other federal agencies.

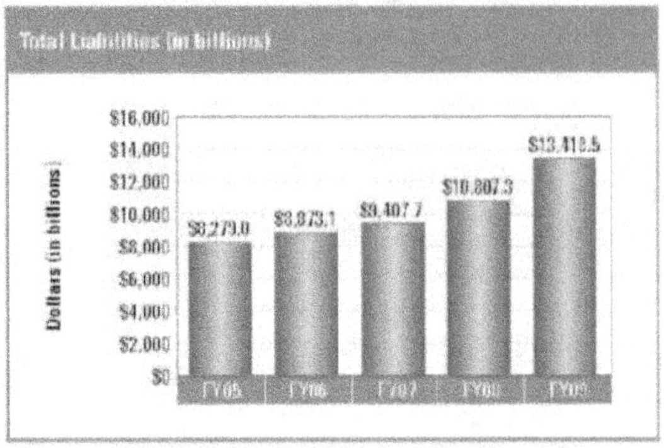

Total liabilities increased by $2.6 trillion from fiscal year 2008 to fiscal year 2009. The majority of the increase is due to borrowings from other federal agencies and debt issued to the public.

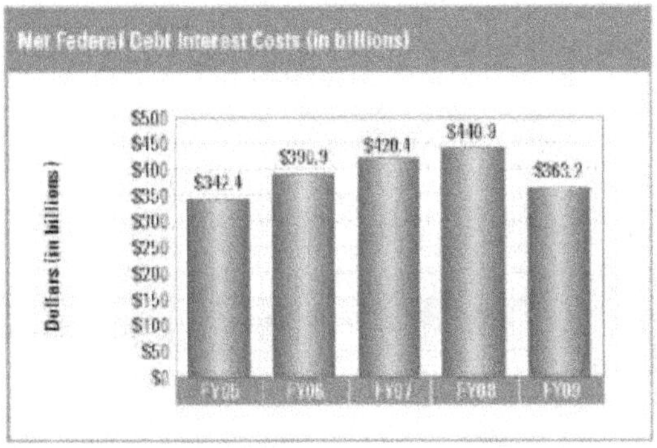

The decrease of $77.7 billion in net interest paid on the federal debt is due to the decrease in the average interest rate for debt held by federal entities and federal debt held by the public.

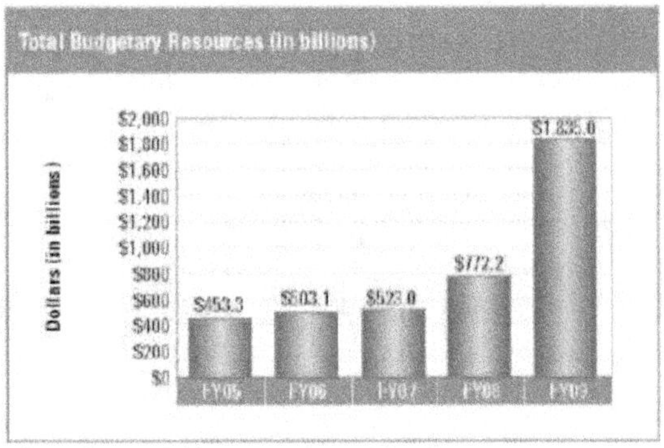

The majority of the increase in total budgetary resources for fiscal year 2009 is due to Troubled Asset Relief Program (TARP) activity and additional investments in the Government-Sponsored Enterprises.

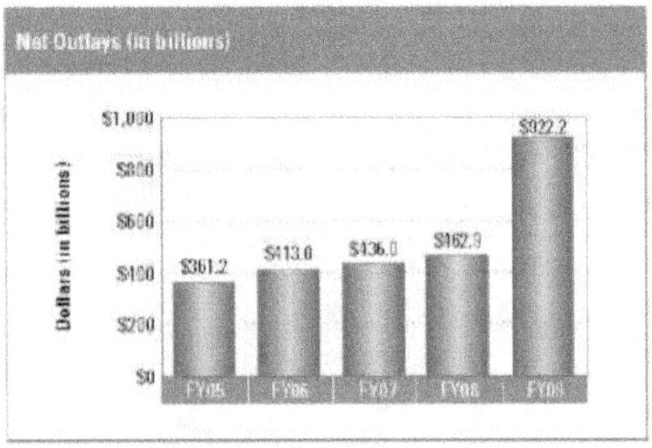

The majority of the $459.3 billion increase in net outlays was due to Troubled Asset Relief Program (TARP) activity and additional investments in the Government-Sponsored Enterprises.

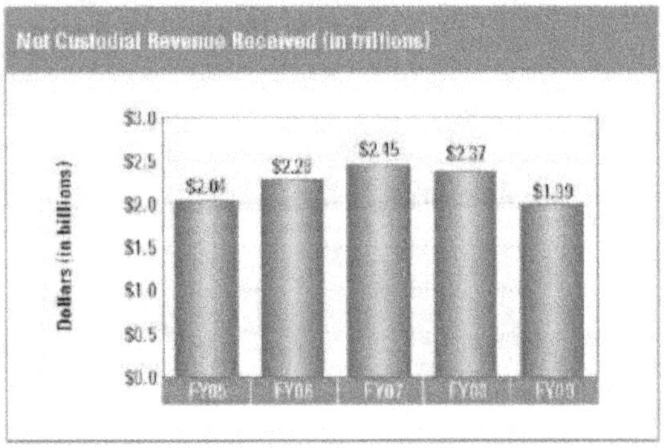

Net custodial revenue collected on behalf of the U.S. Government decreased by $379.3 billion. This decrease can be contributed to the weakened economic conditions that existed during fiscal year 2009.

Appendix 1 – MD&A Best Practices – Current Federal MD&A Standards

Current Federal MD&A Standards

FASAB Standards

Current MD&A standards and concepts provide guidance and establish minimum requirements.[6] SFFAC 3 provides the basic MD&A concepts while SFFAS 15 establishes the requirement that an entity present an MD&A with required components in its general purpose federal financial report (GPFFR).

SFFAC 3 provides that MD&A should address the entity's program and financial performance measures, financial statements, systems and controls, compliance with laws and regulations, and actions taken or planned to address problems. The discussion and analysis of these subjects may be based partly on information contained in reports other than the GPFFR. In addition, MD&A also should address significant events, conditions, trends, and contingencies that may affect future operations.[7]

SFFAC 3 notes that financial reports have two key roles: feedback and prediction. Managers have the knowledge and should explain what the report is communicating. MD&A makes the GPFFR understandable.[8] Due to the complexity of the federal government and the lack of user familiarity with federal financial and performance concepts, MD&A may be more important in the federal government than in the private sector.[9] A third key role is that financial reports require the accumulation and compilation of auditable and therefore reliable information, which agencies would not otherwise do, and which results in the agency personnel gaining an understanding of their agency's financial condition and operations that they would not otherwise have.[10]

SFFAC 3 lists five subjects an MD&A should address:[11]

1) the entity's structure, mission, goals, and objectives, with indicators of its performance;
2) actions taken or planned to improve performance, when appropriate;
3) the financial statements;
4) systems, internal controls and legal compliance, including corrective action taken or planned; and
5) the future effects of existing, currently-known demands, risks, uncertainties, events, conditions and trends. MD&A may also address the possible future effects of anticipated future demands, events,

---

[6] The table in Appendix A provides a comparison of MD&A concepts, standards, and requirements from SFFAC 3, SFFAS 15, and Circular A-136, and shows the similarities and differences between these documents. It illustrates the brevity of SFFAS 15.
[7] SFFAC 3, par. 1.
[8] SFFAC 3, pars. 3-5.
[9] SFFAC 3, par. 7.
[10] SFFAC 3, par. 17.
[11] SFFAC 3, par. 9.

> conditions, trends, etc. that management believes would be important to the reader of the report. MD&A should explain future effects if there is a reasonable prospect of occurrence.[12] "Future effects" should be quantified, if possible, and ranges are useful in discussing future effects.[13]

SFFAS 15, the FASAB's MD&A standard, establishes the basic requirements for an MD&A and requires that each of the above subjects be addressed.[14]

In addition, SFFAC 3 explains that the MD&A should discuss each topic even if basic information on that topic is in a non-GPFFR report. The MD&A concepts included referencing such material.

Regarding financial statement analysis – item 3 in the paragraph above – SFFAC 3, the MD&A concepts, provides that management should give readers the benefit of its understanding from both a short- and long-term perspective. Management should discuss the significance and potential effect of variations in assets, liabilities, costs, revenues, obligations, and outlays; of particular balances and amounts in the financial statements; and of stewardship information.[15] The MD&A should explain significant variations from prior years, from the budget, and from plans, and the potential effect of these factors, of changed circumstances, and of expected future trends.[16] The discussion should include only those variations of potential interest to readers who are not part of agency management.

Not all material changes are sufficiently important to be included in MD&A. Thus, the MD&A should summarize the most important items, explain the relevant causes and efforts, and place them in context.[17]

Regarding performance, SFFAC 3 calls for the entity to explain what it does and how well it is doing it. The MD&A should provide information readers need to gauge success. It should explain how the entity measures success and what the measures show.[18]

To assess a government entity's performance, readers need to know more than simple financial information.[19] Reporting performance in government is different than in the private sector.[20] The financial statement analysis should answer questions such as: What is the entity's financial position and condition? How did this come about? MD&A

---

[12] SFFAC 3, par. 34.
[13] SFFAC 3, par. 35-36.
[14] SFFAS 15, pars. 2-4.
[15] SFFAC 3, 26-7.
[16] SFFAC 3. par. 14.
[17] SFFAC 3, 26-7.
[18] SFFAC 3, par. 11.
[19] SFFAC 3, par. 13.
[20] SFFAC 3, par. 42.

should relate the strategic plan to the entity's results, include both positive and negative results, explain what needs to be done and what is planned, and note the limitations of performance reporting.[21]

Regarding systems and controls, the MD&A should tell the reader whether the internal accounting and administrative controls are adequate.[22] The GPFFR may include summaries of information about systems, internal legal compliance from other reports, e.g., FMFIA and FFMIA reports, or incorporate them by reference. The MD&A, in turn, should discuss the most important aspects of this information.[23]

OMB Circular A-136

OMB Circular A-136, *Financial Reporting Requirements*,[24] defines the form and content for the federal agency PARs and Pilot Program reports required to be submitted to the OMB and the Congress.[25] Circular A-136 provides a framework within which individual agencies have flexibility to provide information useful to the Congress, agency managers, and the public.[26]

Circular A-136 MD&A Provisions

The MD&A provisions of Circular A-136 cite SFFAC 3 and SFFAS 15. Thus, the Circular A-136 requires MD&A sections wherein the entity is to discuss and analyze:

1) mission and organizational structure
2) performance goals, objectives, and results
3) financial statements and stewardship information
4) systems, controls and legal compliance.[27]

Also as in SFFAS 15 (par. 3), Circular A-136 includes the requirement for forward-looking information.

Circular A-136 MD&A Performance Reporting

In addition, Circular A-136 includes extensive MD&A instructions with respect to performance reporting. The Circular provides that the MD&A should include (in no

---

[21] SFFAC 3, par. 45-9.
[22] SFFAC 3, par. 15.
[23] SFFAC 3, pars. 18-22.
[24] June 10, 2009.
[25] See the Chief Financial Officers Act of 1990 ("CFO Act") (Pub. L. 101 – 576), as amended by the Reports Consolidation Act of 2000 (Pub. L. 106-531); the Accountability of Tax Dollars Act of 2002 ("ATDA") (Pub. L. 107–289); and Annual Management Reports under the Government Corporations Control Act (31 U.S.C. § 9101 et seq.). The PARs and AFRs are in addition to the reports submitted to OMB for purposes of monitoring budget execution.
[26] See Circular A-136, Section I.1, *Guide to the Circular.*
[27] Circular A-136, Section II.2.4, Scope.

specific order) highlights of performance goals and results (positive and negative) related to and consistent with major goals and objectives in the entity's strategic and performance plans, including trend data where available. These performance highlights should:

1) provide a clear, objective picture of the entity's program results compared to its goals and objectives;
2) indicate the extent to which its programs are achieving their intended goals and objectives, and explain performance trends;
3) discuss the strategies and resources the entity uses to achieve its performance goals;
4) evaluate the significance of underlying factors that may have affected the reported performance. These may include information about factors that are substantially outside the entity's control as well as information about factors over which the entity has significant control;
5) include an explanation of plans and timelines to improve performance where targets were not met;
6) summarize the procedures management has designed and followed to provide reasonable assurance that reported performance information is relevant and reliable; and
7) discuss important limitations and difficulties associated with performance measurement and reporting should be noted to the extent relevant.[28]

Circular A-136 encourages entities to provide information in the PAR that helps the reader assess the relative efficiency and effectiveness of entity programs/operations. Efficiency is defined as the ratio of an "effective or useful" outcome or output to the total input resources of a system. Effectiveness means having an intended or expected effect.[29]

Entities are instructed to strive to articulate efficiency and effectiveness by developing and reporting objective measures that, to the extent possible, indicate results achieved and relate major goals and objectives in their strategic plan to cost categories (i.e., responsibility segments) presented in the entity's statement of net cost. Entities should be engaged in strategic management, including recognizing that the dual objectives of and the occasional trade-offs between efficiency and effectiveness (e.g., the most effective solution or process is not always the most efficient, nor is the most efficient always the most effective). Entities should focus on tracking and reporting the most appropriate and meaningful measures that show program effectiveness, efficiency, and results.

---

[28] Circular A-136, Section II.2.6, *Performance Goals, Objectives, and Results.*
[29] Ibid.

Appendix 1 – MD&A Best Practices – Current Federal MD&A Standards

Circular A-136 MD&A Financial Statement Analysis

With respect to financial statement analysis, Circular A-136 incorporates SFFAS 15 paragraphs. [30] Thus, MD&A should help users understand the entity's financial results, position and condition conveyed in the principal financial statements. The MD&A should include comparisons of the current year to the prior year and should provide an analysis of the agency's overall financial position and results of operations to assist users in assessing whether that financial position has improved or deteriorated as a result of the year's activities. It should give users the benefit of management's understanding of the:

1) Major changes in types or amounts of assets, liabilities, costs, revenues, obligations, and outlays;
2) Relevance of particular balances and amounts shown in the principal financial statements, particularly if relevant to important financial management issues; and
3) Entity's stewardship information.

This section should also include a discussion of key financial-related measures emphasizing financial trends and assess financial operations.

Circular A-136 MD&A Systems and Controls

Circular A-136 requires agencies to provide assurances related to the Federal Managers' Financial Integrity Act (FMFIA) and the Federal Financial Management Improvement Act (FFMIA)[31] in a separate section of the MD&A entitled "Management Assurances." The Circular instructs the agencies that the FMFIA assurance statement should:

1) Provide management's assessment of the effectiveness of the organization's internal controls to support effective and efficient programmatic operations, reliable financial reporting, and compliance with applicable laws and regulations (FMFIA § 2); and whether the financial management systems conform to financial systems requirements (FMFIA § 4).
2) Provide a separate assessment of the effectiveness of the internal controls over financial reporting as a subset of the overall FMFIA assurance statement (i.e., separate paragraph within the FMFIA Assurance Statement).
3) Include a summary of material weaknesses (FMFIA § 2) and non-conformances (FMFIA § 4), and a summary of corrective actions to resolve the material weaknesses and non-conformances. Illustrative assurance statements and further guidance on corrective action plans

[30] Circular A-136, Section II.2.7, "Analysis of the Entity's Financial Statements and Stewardship Information."
[31] Pub.L.No.104-208.

can be found in the CFOC Implementation Guide, Management's Responsibility for Internal Control, Appendix A, Internal Control over Financial Reporting located at: (http://www.cfoc.gov/documents/Impementation_Guide_for_OMB_Circular_A-123.pdf).

Management is also directed to include its FFMIA compliance assessment in this section. FFMIA requires management to assess the organization's compliance with Federal financial management systems requirements, standards promulgated by FASAB, and the U.S. Standard General Ledger (USSGL) at the transaction level. Further guidance on the financial systems requirements can be found in OMB Circular A-127, *Financial Management Systems.* Circular A-11, Part 2, Section 52, *Information on Financial Management* outlines requirements for agency's plans for bringing its systems into substantial compliance.

Management is to review its FMFIA assurance statements and its FFMIA compliance determination for consistency with the findings specified in the annual financial statement audit report(s). The Office of Inspector General or auditor is to compare material weaknesses disclosed during the audit with those material weaknesses reported in the agency's FMFIA report and document any differences. The reports could, in fact be different, but they should not be in direct conflict. When conflicting discrepancies exist, it is management's responsibility to ensure that outstanding issues are appropriately reported.

A review of agency reporting reveals some noteworthy aspects of FMFIA reporting. What appears to be happening is that management reports material weaknesses in internal control using criteria different than the auditors use to determine material weaknesses and system non-conformances in the accounting and financial reporting systems. The result is that some of the management-determined material weaknesses are different than what the auditor reports and some are the same. However, no instances were found where the auditor reported that a material weakness in internal control in financial systems that management did not report.

The review found different results for FFMIA than for FMFIA. Several instances were found where the auditor reported non-compliance with the FFMIA but management felt that the agency complied. Management frequently tried to justify its position rather than state what it will do to remove the auditor's finding.

Circular A-136 MD&A Other Provisions

In addition, Circular A-136 affords management the discretion to include a summary in the MD&A of other information, initiatives, and issues it identifies. This could include summarizing entity progress in implementing key administration management initiatives.[32]

Circular A-136 requires the MD&A to include a section articulating the limitations of the principal financial statements, and provides the specific wording.[33]

Circular A-136 Non-MD&A PAR Sections

Circular A-136 directs that Sections 2, 3 and 4 of the PAR be for performance reporting, financial statements, and other accompanying information, respectively. The instructions for performance reporting in Circular A-136 are taken from Circular A-11, Section 230, *Preparing and submitting the Annual Performance Report, the Performance Portion of a Performance and Accountability Report*. Circular A-11 takes precedent if there is any inconsistency between Circulars A-11 and A-136.[34] Agencies are instructed to refer to Circular A-11 for a comprehensive discussion on performance. The annual performance report required by GPRA provides information on an agency's actual performance and progress in achieving the goals in its strategic plan and performance budget.

Agencies prepare one annual performance report for a fiscal year. For most agencies, this is the "Performance Section" of its PAR. For those agencies participating in the pilot, the APR is to accompany the Congressional Budget Justification (CBJ).

---

[32] OMB Circular A-136, Section II.2.9.
[33] OMB Circular A-136, Section II.2.10.
[34] OMB Circular A-136, Section II.3.1, General, fn. 20.

MD&A Task Group

Name	Federal Agency
Regina Kearney, Chairperson	Office of Management and Budget
Carmen Pearlstein	Commerce Department
Shirley Watt	National Science Foundation
Lisa Hemmer	Department of Homeland Security
Cynthia Simpson	Labor Department
Scott Bell	Treasury Department
Joseph Donovan	Labor Department
Melissa Evans	Department of Homeland Security
Mike Swanchara	General Services Administration
Molly Dawson	Department of Health and Human Services
Charles Fox	Government Accountability Office
Kevin McFadden	KPMG
Richard Fontenrose	Federal Accounting Standards Advisory Board

www.ingramcontent.com/pod-product-compliance
Lightning Source LLC
Chambersburg PA
CBHW080300180526
45167CB00006B/2611
* 9 7 8 1 5 0 5 5 5 7 4 5 9 *